CHARLES KINGSLEY'S LANDSCAPE

Ah, now it fades! and I must pine
Again for that dread country crystalline,
Where the blank field and the still-standing tree
Were bright and fearful presences to me.

Edwin Muir, *Horses*

Also by Susan Chitty:

The Diary of a Fashion Model
White Huntress
My Life and Horses
The Woman Who Wrote Black Beauty
The Beast and the Monk
(*A Life of Charles Kingsley*)

CHARLES KINGSLEY'S LANDSCAPE

Susan Chitty

DAVID & CHARLES

NEWTON ABBOT LONDON NORTH POMFRET (VT) VANCOUVER

FOR A.K.

ISBN 0 7153 7215 7
Library of Congress Catalog Card Number 76–8619

Set in 11 on 13pt Plantin
and printed in Great Britain
by Latimer Trend & Company Ltd Plymouth
for David & Charles (Publishers) Limited
Brunel House Newton Abbot Devon

Published in the United States of America
by David & Charles Inc
North Pomfret Vermont 05053 USA

Published in Canada
by Douglas David & Charles Limited
1875 Welch Street North Vancouver BC

Contents

Acknowledgements:

All the photographs are by Thomas Hinde except for the aerial view of Lundy which was supplied by Knight's Photographers

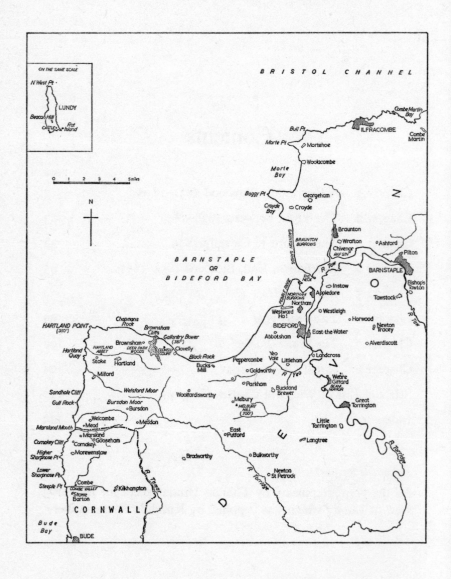

ON THE SAME SCALE

N West Pt ·

LUNDY

Beacon Hill
CASTLE
Rat Island

0 1 2 3 4 5 miles

N

BRISTOL CHANNEL

Combe Martin Bay

ILFRACOMBE

Combe Martin

Bull Pt

Morte Pt

Mortehoe

Woolacombe

Morte Bay

N

Baggy Pt

Georgeham

Croyde Bay

Croyde

Braunton

Wrafton

Ashford

Chivenor
R.A.F. STN.

Pilton

BRAUNTON BURROWS

BARNSTAPLE

Bishop's Tawton

BARNSTAPLE
OR
BIDEFORD BAY

THE NECK

R. Taw

Instow

Appledore

Westleigh

Tawstock

R. Taw

HARTLAND POINT
(350')

Chapmans Rock

Brownsham Cliffs

Gallantry Bower
(387')

PEBBLE RIDGE

NORTHAM BURROWS

Northam

Westward Ho!

BIDEFORD

Abbotsham

East-the-Water

Horwood

Newton Tracey

Hartland Quay

HARTLAND ABBEY

Brownsham

DEER PARK WOODS

CLOVELLY COURT

Clovelly

Black Rock

Peppercombe

Vyo Vale

Littleham

Landcross

Alverdiscott

Stoke

Hartland

Bucks Mill

Goldworthy

R. Yeo

Weare Giffard

BEAM MANOR

Milford

Welsford Moor

Parkham

Buckland Brewer

Great Torrington

Sandhole Cliff

Gull Rock

Bursdon Moor

Bursdon

Woolfardisworthy

Melbury

MELBURY HILL
(700')

Little Torrington

Marsland Mouth

Welcombe

Mead

Marsland
Gooseham

Meddon

East Putford

Langtree

Cornakey Cliff

Cornakey

Morwenstow

Bradworthy

Bulkworthy

E

Higher Sharpnose Pt

R. TAMAR

Newton St Petrock

R. TORRIDGE

Lower Sharpnose Pt

Steeple Pt

Combe
COMBE VALLEY
Stowe Barton

Kilkhampton

R. TORRIDGE

CORNWALL

D

Bude Bay

BUDE

Chapter 1

A Devonshire Boyhood 1831-1836

Charles Kingsley was born in Devonshire in 1819 and always considered himself a man of Devon. Although he ceased to reside in the county at the age of seventeen and did not spend a holiday there after the age of thirty-six, to him Devonshire was always 'the beloved country'. He claimed that to think of the West Country made him weep. 'I am,' he once wrote to his mother, 'perhaps the only Englishman I ever met who has continually the true *Heimweh* homesickness of the Swiss and the High-landers.' During the nervous breakdowns of the early part of his life he constantly returned to Devon to be 're-magnetised'.

This love for the West, Kingsley was convinced, was fed to him in his mother's womb. The Rev Charles Kingsley, senior, and his wife Mary lived at Holne rectory, an old cream-coloured house tucked into a fold of Dartmoor on its southern edge. The rectory still stands, with the green Dart valley fanning out before it and the grey gauntness of the moor forming a rampart behind. It was the moor that Mrs Kingsley, a poet in secret, loved, she took daily walks up on to Leigh Tor and then, deafened by the wind howling through rocks as tall as castles, would plunge into the silence of Holne Chase where the gnarled moss-laden trees descended steeply to the river. She was convinced that by doing this she could communicate her love for the place to her unborn child.

Kingsley's parents left Holne when he was only six weeks old, taking with them a local girl, Annie Simpson, who acted as his

7

nursemaid for some years. Kingsley's father had entered the
Church late in life, when his money gave out. Before that he had
led the life of a country gentleman with sporting tastes. Holne
had been only his second curacy and he was now offered a slightly
better one at Burton-on-Trent. For the next six years he was to
lead a nomadic life, moving from curacy to curacy, finally settling
at the haunted rectory at Barnack on the edge of the Fens where
he was rector. In 1830 the son of the Bishop of Peterborough
took over the living from him and Charles Kingsley, senior,
returned to Devonshire, unemployed and suffering from the ague
(malaria). Luckily one of his friends was Sir James Hamlyn
Williams, who had succeeded his father as third baronet in 1829.
Sir James, full of ferocity against the Tories, gruff but generous,
lived at Clovelly Court. In 1831 a curate was needed at Clovelly,
and Mr Kingsley was appointed to the post. The following
year the rector died and Sir James presented the living to his
curate.

Charles Kingsley was twelve years old when he first saw
Clovelly, that incredible North Devon fishing village whose main
street consists of a flight of cobbled steps following the route of
an old watercourse. He came to it, as one should, by sea. His
father had decided that the most economical way to transport his
family and furniture west was by ship across Bideford Bay.
Clovelly is 40 miles from Ilfracombe by land, but the direct
route across the water is shorter.

In an article he wrote for *Fraser's Magazine* twenty years later,
Kingsley described his arrival, 'crawling up the paved stairs in-
accessible to cart or carriage, which are flatteringly denominated
Clovelly Street, behind me a sheer descent to the pier and bay
200 feet below, and in front, another 100 feet above, a green
amphitheatre of oak and ash, shutting out all but a narrow slip
of sky, across which a mist was crawling. Suddenly a hot gleam
of sunshine fell upon the white cottages, with their grey steaming
roofs, and bright green railings, and on the tree-fuchsias and

gaudy dahlias in the little scraps of garden courtyard, calling out the rich faint odour of the verbenas and jessamines, and, alas! out of the herring-heads and tails also as they lay in the rivulet; and lighting up the wings of the gorgeous butterflies, almost unknown in our colder clime, which fluttered from woodland down to garden.'

Clovelly was at this time totally unknown to the outside world, a place apart. The only other writer who attempted to describe it in the middle years of the century was Dickens who published what he described as a 'nouvelette' about it, entitled *A Message from the Sea*, in the Christmas 1860 issue of his magazine *All the Year Round*. 'From the sea-beach to the cliff top, the two irregular rows of white houses, placed opposite to one another, and twisting here and there, rose like the sides of a long succession of crooked ladders, and you climbed up the village by the staves between, some six feet wide or so, and made of sharp irregular stones. The old pack saddle, long laid aside in most parts of England . . . flourished here intact. Strings of pack-horses and pack-donkeys toiled slowly up the staves of the ladders, bearing fish, and coal, and such other cargo as was unshipping at the pier from the dancing fleet of village boats, and from two or three little coasting traders. As the beasts of burden ascended laden, or descended light, they got so lost at intervals in the floating clouds of village smoke, that they seemed to dive down some of the village chimneys and come to the surface again far off.'

Another visitor, thirty years later, enjoyed watching the donkeys. Arthur Norway,* sitting on the balcony of the New Inn, which still stands halfway up the street, described them 'limping from the quay, straying into the cool shade of every open doorway which they pass, while women come out and hang over the green balconies and scold and chatter at the luckless driver, who defends himself in his slow western speech, and at last with many thwackings sets the head of the poor patient

* Arthur H. Norway, *Highways and Byways of Devon and Cornwall*.

9

donkey straight again, and goes up three steps more when the same process is repeated'.

The rectory stood above Clovelly on the left of the road that ascends from the village. It was a tall eighteenth-century house, rather like a doll's house with four rooms symmetrically arranged on each of its three floors. It was set among trees with a lawn and circular drive in front and a coach house and stables near the entrance gate. A bank rising at one side was carpeted with wild daffodils in the spring and surmounted by a huge oak tree, in which the children could build tree houses.

There were five boys and a girl in the Kingsley family. Only a year separated Charles from Herbert and Herbert from Gerald; George, Charlotte* and Henry had followed after an interval of five years. Charles was a somewhat nervous and solitary boy with an over-developed conscience. Strong feelings of guilt had been apparent in his make-up since the age of four, when, on being told that his mother had forgiven him for some minor transgression he cried, 'It isn't mamma's forgiveness I want, but God's.' But if he was in awe of God, he was also in awe of his father, before whom he had to recite lessons in Latin at a set time each day. It was no doubt while groping for words in front of the rector's desk that Charles developed the stutter that was to plague him for the rest of his days. As a small child he had suffered from frequent attacks of croup and it took all the skill of an old nurse, Betsy Knowles, who had been with his father's family for years, and Annie Simpson, of Holne, to nurse him through them. These devoted women also had to combat the effects of the drugs that were recommended for croup. Kingsley was later to declare that the massive doses of calomel (mercurous chloride) that he was given for so-called 'biliousness' inhibited the growth of his jaw and increased his tendency to stammer, or 'hesitate', as he preferred to call it.

* Charlotte married a rector of Clovelly and, as Mrs J. M. Chanter, wrote *Ferny Combes. A ramble after ferns in the glens and valleys of Devonshire*, and a novel, *Over the Cliffs*.

The life of the Kingsley family, and indeed of the entire village, was dominated by the lord of the manor and patron of the living, Sir James Hamlyn Williams. His fine eighteenth-century mansion, Clovelly Court, was on the far side of the road from the rectory. It stood on the cliffs and commanded a view of Bideford Bay from its parapeted terrace. The house had been built in the Early Gothic Revival style by Zachary Hamlyn, the founder of the family fortunes, who died in 1759. His son had classicised the house, leaving only one Gothic feature, the main enttrance, with its clustered shafts and Perpendicular tracery. Of more interest to the young Kingsley was the Tudor part at the back of the house, that had been the home of the Cary family for generations.

A great deal older than even the oldest parts of Clovelly Court was the church of All Saints which crouched directly behind the great house, almost in its shadow. The church was full of monuments to the Carys, going back to Robert Cary who died in 1540.

These reminders of the seagoing family, and the sight from his tree house of the endless blue stretching westwards, filled young Charles Kingsley's head with dreams about the West Indies and the Spanish Main. His mother had spent her childhood in Barbados and had often told him of her home, Farley Hall, with its pillared portico and famous bearded fig tree. In her sitting room at the rectory there was a cabinet full of shells that she had picked up on the beaches of that sunlit island, and in his father's library was the collection of books she had inherited: 'lordly folios on whose maps many a sturdy coastline dwindled into dots —full many a line of dots went stumbling on to perish at the foot of pregnant nothingness. Volume on volume of famous voyagers —Dampier, Rogers, Shelrocke, Byron, Cook and grand old Esqumeling—the Froissart of the Buccaneers—and respectable Captain Charles Johnson, deeply interested and very properly shocked by "the Robberies and Murders of the most Notorious Pirates" .'*

* Mary Kingsley's introduction to George Kingsley's *Notes on Sport and Travel.*

In books like these he read stories of the 'old sea heroes', Sir Walter Ralegh and Sir Richard Grenville, Drake and Hawkins, Carleill and Cavendish, Cumberland, Preston and Frobisher. He longed to see for himself such wonders as the Sargasso Sea, that 'sunken Atlantic Continent', and relive 'the memorable day when Columbus' ship plunged her bows into the tangled ocean meadow, and the sailors were ready to mutiny, fearing hidden shoals, ignorant that they had four miles of blue water beneath their keel'.*

For the time being, however, the piece of sea that lay below his father's front door was sufficient to keep him occupied. The Rev Charles Kingsley took an active interest in the lives of his sea-faring parishioners. To him Devonshire men with their courage, their physical beauty and their vivid modes of expression were a race apart from the 'South Saxon clods', and he spent much time down on the quay with the fishermen. The rector could steer a boat, hoist and lower a sail, 'shoot' a herring net and haul a seine with the best of them; and when the herring fleet put to sea, whatever the weather, he would hurry off 'down street' with his whole family to give a short service and join in the singing of the old Prayer Book version of the 121st Psalm:

> Though storms be sudden, and waters deep
> Thy Guardian will not sleep.†

Clovelly's little harbour was a busy place in those days. It was situated on the western rim of Bideford Bay, so that from it you could see, looking east, the white sand of Braunton and, dimly, the high ground of Exmoor above Ilfracombe. The harbour basin was not silted up, as it is today, and when the fishing fleet was in visitors at the Red Lion Inn on the quay could see 'a forest of masts' from the bar room window. The young Kingsley loved to be out in the bay when the 'herring boats were hastily

---

* Charles Kingsley, *At Last.*
† Brady and Tate, *Metric Psalms.*

hauling their nets—you could see the fish sparkling like flakes of silver as they came up over the gunwale'. Fishing in these waters was a dangerous business, for storms could blow up suddenly in Bideford Bay. Charles had been at Clovelly only a year when he witnessed what was probably the worst fishing disaster in the history of the place. On the night of 4 October 1831 'the old bay darkened with the grey columns of the water-spouts, stalking across the waves before the northern gale; and the tiny herring-boats fleeing from their nets right for the breakers, hoping for more mercy even from those iron walls of rock than from the pitiless howling waste of spray behind them; and that merry beach beside the town was covered with shrieking women and old men, casting themselves on the pebbles in fruitless agonies of prayer, as corpse after corpse swept up at the feet of wife and child, till . . . a single dawn saw upwards of sixty widows and orphans weeping over those who had gone out the night before in the fulness of strength and courage.'* Thirty-one Clovelly sailors and pilots were drowned that night. The Rev Charles Kingsley was deeply concerned for the families left behind. He was the chairman of a committee set up at Bridge Hall, Bideford, for the distribution of funds to them.†

The dangers of Bideford Bay did not discourage young Charles from venturing upon it himself. He early discovered 'the maddening excitement' of managing his own small trawler, but it was shells rather than fish that interested him. Bideford Bay was (and still is) famous for its shells and both his parents were keen conchologists. The Rev Charles Kingsley would often drag a trawl net along the bottom of the bay with the help of his three older boys. Sometimes the whole family, accompanied by Susannah Blackmore, the new nursemaid from Parracombe, would hire a boat to take them to one of the beaches on the bay

---

* Charles Kingsley, *Prose Idylls*.
† The handwritten minutes of the meetings of the committee are in the possession of Kenneth Goodridge of Plymouth, who has kindly supplied copies of them.

where shells were abundant. Rich hunting grounds were Braunton Sands and the rocky area above Morte Sands (now known as Woolacombe Sands). 'Every gully and creek there among the rocks is yellow, but not with sand. Those are shells; the sweepings of the ocean bed for miles around, piled there, millions upon millions, yards deep, in every stage of destruction. There they lie grinding to dust; and every gale brings in fresh myriads.'*

Nets of shells from these expeditions were lugged to the doorstep of a doctor in Bideford whom Kingsley always described as 'poor dear old opium-eating Dr Turton'. Dr Turton had become an expert on shells when conchology and microscopic inspection were still in their infancy and was one of the first people to introduce the Linnaean system of classification to the British public. Between 1802 and 1806 he edited a seven volume work described as *A general system of nature, translated from Gmelin's last edition of the Systema Naturae (of Linnaeus).* He devoted the last years of his life to a book on shells which he published in 1831: *A Manual of the land and fresh-water shells of the British Islands arranged according to the more modern systems of classification & described from perfect specimens in the author's cabinet with coloured plates of every species.*

Each of the specimens so exquisitely illustrated in the 152-page book was indeed to be found in his private collection. Kingsley was active in helping Turton collect shells. He searched not only for sea shells but also for land ones, and spent many hours poking about among rotten leaves in the woods above Clovelly looking for snails.

When Dr Turton died in 1835, he left his shells to William Clark of Bath. They ended up with the John Gwyn Jeffreys collection at the United States National Museum at Washington. In 1840, a second edition of Turton's shell manual appeared, heavily edited by John Edward Gray. Though twice as long, it omitted several of the original shells on the grounds that Turton

* Charles Kingsley, *Prose Idylls.*

14

could not possibly have found them, as he claimed, in the British Isles. In 1849 two naturalists, Forbes and Henley, paid Turton the compliment of naming a genus of bivalve *Turtonia* in his honour, but rather spoilt the effect by adding, 'Turton could not always be relied on in published statements.'

The vast headland of Hartland Point forms the western boundary of Bideford Bay; 350ft high, of almost sheer black rock, it butts out into the full fury of the Atlantic. It is the tip of a large peninsula of wild moorland, the western side of which runs down to the Cornish border, broken by a series of deep inlets—known locally as combes—such as Spekes Mill Mouth, Welcombe Mouth and Marsland Mouth.

This beautiful coastline of the Hartland peninsula was the scene of frequent shipwrecks. Kingsley witnessed one of these as a boy:

One morning I can remember well how we watched from the Hartland Cliffs a great barque, which came drifting and rolling in before the western gale, while we followed her up the coast, parsons and sportsmen, farmers and Preventive men, with the Manby's mortar lumbering behind us in a cart, through stone gaps and track ways, from headland to headland . . . The maddening excitement of expectation as she ran wildly towards the cliffs at our feet, and then sheered off again inexplicably; her foremast and bowsprit, I recollect, were gone short off by the deck; a few rags of sail fluttered from her main and mizen. But with all straining of eyes and glass we could discern no sign of men on board; . . . and then, how a boat's crew of Clovelly fishermen appeared in view, and how we watched the little black speck crawling and struggling up in the teeth of the gale, till, when the ship had rounded a point into smooth water, she seized on her like some tiny spider on a huge unwieldy fly; and how one still smaller speck showed aloft on the mainyard, and another—and then the desperate efforts to get the topsail set—and how we saw it tear out of their hands again and again and again; and almost fancied we could hear the thunder of its flappings above the roar of the gale, and the mountains of surf which made the rocks ring beneath our feet;—and how we stood silent, shuddering, expecting every moment to see whirled into the sea from the plunging

15

jerk of those same tiny black specks, in each of which was a living human soul, with sad women praying for him at home! . . . I recollect our literally warping ourselves down to the beach, holding on by rocks and posts . . . A sudden turn of the clouds let in a wild gleam of moonshine upon the white leaping heads of the breakers, and on the pyramid of the Black Church Rock, which stands in summer in such calm grandeur gazing down on the smiling bay, with the white sand of Braunton and the red cliffs of Portledge shining through its two vast arches; and against a slab of rock on the right, for years after discoloured with her paint, lay the ship, rising slowly on every surge, to drop again with a piteous crash as the wave fell back from the cliff and dragged the roaring pebbles back with it under the coming wall of foam. You have heard of ships that at the last moment cry aloud like living things in agony? I heard it then, as the stumps of her masts rocked and reeled in her, and every plank and joint strained and screamed with the dreadful tension.

Most of the roads across the Hartland peninsula ran along the bare windy ridges of moors like Bursdon, Welsford, Hendon and Tosberry, but every now and again they descended to a valley where all was miraculously green and still, and it was in this contrast that the fascination of the landscape lay. All the Kingsley boys had stout Exmoor ponies to ride across this splendid country, ponies that were wise enough to avoid the treacherous bogs that could swallow up a horse and his rider, and they were free to wander where they liked.

It was the archaeological sites scattered about the peninsula that particularly interested young Charles and early fired his historical imagination. One of the most famous of these lay only a mile from his home: Clovelly Dykes was a series of grand earthworks covering 20 acres, among the largest in England. It consisted of three banks and ditches, the banks being about 20ft high and the ditches about 25yd wide. On the east was a crescent-shaped outwork with a double bank and ditch which was possibly the entrance. Kingsley considered that these were the remains of a Roman hill fort, but most modern authorities attribute it to

Early Iron Age Celts who were attempting to keep out Roman invaders from the sea around 100 BC.

Kingsley was equally fascinated by another ruin that he also took to be Roman, in this case a villa on the west coast, 'tumbling into the sea, tesselated pavements, baths and all'. It was perhaps that ruined villa which first gave Kingsley his feeling for the past. He imagined rather surprisingly, 'the strange work' that went on 'in that lonely nook, among a seraglio of dark Celtic beauties'.* He was in fact almost certainly mistaken in supposing that the ruin was a Roman one, for the Romans barely penetrated North Devon. He probably referred to Embury Beacon, a second-century Iron Age fort near Welcombe Mouth, the ramparts of which are now three-quarters fallen into the sea. Kingsley's obsession with the luxurious wickedness of ancient Rome was eventually to find expression in his first historical novel, *Hypatia*, a story about a beautiful female philosopher living in fourth-century Alexandria under Roman rule, a lush tale complete with gladiatorial fights and Christians being thrown to the lions.

Kingsley's father was a keen sportsman and brought up his sons to make full use of the splendid hunting ground that lay at their door. There were fine trout to be caught in the Torridge by those who were on good terms with the owners of riparian rights, and at both flood and ebb tides bass, pollock, conger, bull huss and dog fish could be caught off the rocks of the Western combes. Even when Charles was very young he used to be set before the keeper on his pony to follow his father on shooting expeditions, and in his teens he learnt to bring down rabbits and woodcock with his gun on the moors. But the best sport of all was hunting the cunning Hartland foxes, and there were plenty on the moors around Clovelly for the followers of the North Devon Hounds to pursue.

Like most fox hunters, Kingsley liked foxes, and once described coming upon one unaware: 'A fox it is indeed; a great

* Charles Kingsley, *Prose Idylls*.

dog-fox, as red as the fir-stems between which he glides. And yet his legs are black with fresh peat stains. He is a hunted fox: but he has not been up long.'* To chase such a creature on horseback across the Devonshire uplands he considered one of life's greatest joys. 'How the panting cavalcade rose and fell on the huge mile-long waves of that vast heather sea . . . and how the sandstone rattled and flew beneath their feet, as the great horses, like Homer's of old, "devoured up the plain" . . . and how they swept down the flat valley, rounding crag and headland . . . along the narrow strip of sand and rushes.' He loved to hear 'the sound of his own horse-hoofs . . . as they swept through the fragrant heather blossoms . . . tossing them out in a rosy shower'.

Kingsley was entirely educated in the West Country. Perhaps because of his precarious health, he did not go to school until he was twelve. For a short time he went to a small preparatory school at 34 Richmond Terrace, Bristol, run by the Rev William Knight. What Kingsley was *taught* there seems to have made little impression on him, but something he *saw* remained with him for the rest of his life. By chance he was a witness of the terrible riots of 1831 that resulted from the refusal of the House of Lords to pass the Second Reform Bill. He never forgot the sight of the howling mob of drunken louts, looting and burning everything in their path.

Rather surprisingly, Kingsley was not sent on to one of the major public schools, but to a small grammar school at Helston in Cornwall. It was run by the Rev Derwent Coleridge, a son of the poet, and was housed in an early seventeenth-century terrace house at the bottom of the famous curving main street of Helston, later moving to larger premises at the top of the town.

For Kingsley the school had three great advantages: it allowed its pupils a great deal of freedom, it possessed an excellent library (for Coleridge was a distinguished scholar) and one of its two assistant masters was C. A. Johns, later famous as the

* Charles Kingsley, *Prose Idylls*.

18

author of *Flowers of the Field*. Kingsley became a close friend of Johns and throughout his teens the study of natural history was a consuming passion. He became a keen collector of birds' eggs and geological specimens, but above all he collected, pressed and classified flowers. Long hours were spent on the Lizard and along the oak-fringed banks of the Helford estuary. School holidays were devoted to an equally exact study of the flora of the Clovelly area and careful comparisons were made, as is shown in a letter to his mother written on 16 May 1835:

> ... Dry me as much spurge as you can—as much bird's nest orchis, and plenty of tway-blade, of which there are quantities in the long walk—all the *Arabis* to be found; woodruff, Marsh marigold, and cockle.
>
> Give my love to Emily Wellesley, and ask her to dry me some Adoxa. The plant in the moors is in flower now. *Menyanthes trifoliata* is its name, and we have found it here long ago. I question whether that is really *Arabis stricta, hirsuta* it is very likely to be. If it is *stricta*, it is a most noble prize; but Mr. C. wrong-names his plants dreadfully, between you and I. If you go to Bragela you will find a very large red-stalked spurge, *Euphorbia amygdaloides* growing by the path, before you enter the wood, as you come up from the beach—pray dry me some of this. I have found *Spergula subulata, Vicea angustifolia, Asplenium lanceolatum*! ! ! *Scilla verna, Arenaria verna, Teesdalia nudicaulis, Ornithopus perpusillus, Carex strigosa, Carex aeden*, and several others, of all of which I can give Emily specimens. I believe there are only two other habitats for *Asplenium lanceolatum* known.

But Kingsley's interest in nature was not merely physical; it verged on the metaphysical. In a letter written in his youth he described the strange excitement, often culminating in tears, that was aroused in him by the 'beautiful inanimate ... sun and stars, wood and wave'. He practised a kind of pantheism, peopling favourite moorland springs with attendant nymphs and writing poems about them. Of the nymph in *Hypotheses Hypochondraiae* he wrote:

And should she die, her grave should be
Upon the bare top of a sunny hill,
Among the moorlands of her own fair land,
Amid a ring of old and moss-grown stones
In gorse and heather all embosomed,
Above her gentle corse;—the ponderous pile
Would press too rudely on those fairy limbs.
The turf should lightly lie, that marked her home.
A sacred spot it would be—every bird
That came to watch her lone grave should be holy,
The deer should browse around her undisturbed;
The whin bird by, her lonely nest should build
All fearless:

Mountains on mountains rolling—and dark mist
Wrapped itself round the hill tops like a shroud,
When on her grave swept by the moaning wind
Bending the heather bells—then would I come
And watch by her, in silent loneliness,
And smile upon the storm—as knowing well
The lightening's flash would surely turn aside,
Nor mar the lowly mound, where peaceful sleeps
All that gave life and love to one fond heart!

Equally remote was the dwelling of the nymph who guarded
Trehill Well:

There stood a low and ivied roof,
    As gazing rustics tell,
In times of chivalry and song
    'Yclept the holy well.

Above the ivies' branchlets gray
    In glistening clusters shone;
While round the base the grass-blades bright
    And spiry foxglove sprung.

The brambles clung in graceful bands,
    Chequering the old gray stone
With shining leaflets, whose bright face
    In autumn's tinting shone.

The interest of these two poems, which he wrote while still at Helston Grammar School, goes far beyond their literary merit, for it shows how deeply the love of the western landscape had penetrated into the boy's soul. He had in fact constructed for himself a kind of religion of the hills, the cliffs and the sea, and for the next six years was to worship exclusively at the shrine of Nature.

Kingsley was only to discover how essential a part of him the West Country had become when he was forced to leave it. He was sixteen when his father accepted the living at St Luke's Church, Chelsea. The church was a wealthy one, serving the newly built Cadogan estates, and the rector, with four boys to educate, no doubt needed the money. A fine house went with the living, and one of the largest private gardens in London. The Thames was not far away; in those days the Chelsea reach was countrified and Battersea no more than a marsh dotted with windmills.

But none of this could console Kingsley for the loss of Clovelly. He found London ugly, and Londoners also—at any rate those that frequented St Luke's rectory. He described his father's curates as 'dapper young-ladies-preachers' and the charitably inclined young women who assisted his mother in her endless parochial work as 'nothing but ugly splay-footed beings, three-fourths of whom can't sing, and the other quarter sing miles out of tune, with voices like love sick parrots. Confound!!! They have got their heads crammed full of Schools, and district visiting, and baby linen and penny clubs. Confound!!! And go about among the most abominable scenes of filth, wretchedness and indecency, to visit and read the Bible.'

He was entered at King's College, to prepare for entry to Cambridge. For two years he worked at Greek and Latin literature and mathematics, walking up to the West End daily with his head in a book and walking home late to study all evening. He appeared to have no recreations whatsoever, for his father was a low churchman who disapproved of the theatre, music and parties. Charles had few friends; even the companionship of his brothers was denied him, for Herbert had died of rheumatic fever at Helston Grammar School and Gerald had joined the navy.

It was hardly surprising that he became ill. He grew thin and spotty and started to have hallucinations. He was unable to concentrate and it was eventually discovered that he had a seriously congested left lung. Various painful cures were attempted but the one that succeeded was a holiday at Clovelly. He travelled there by sea and his joy at returning to the place shines through a letter written to his mother on 24 August 1837:

> . . . We had a calm and delightful passage down, with a bright sun and a smooth sea—just what you would have enjoyed . . . I am exceedingly well here—quite a different being since I came, and my only fear is that I shall not stay long enough. I wish it were possible for me to stay a month or six weeks, and then come back to King's College quite fat and fresh from the country, and all ready for work . . . Tell Charlotte that I am getting her some sea-weeds, and that we are going to Braunton, and will get her some shells . . . the dear old place looks quite natural, and yet somehow it is like a dream when I think of the total revulsion that two days' journey has made in me, and how I seem like some spirit in the metempsychosis which has suddenly passed back, out of a new life, into one which it bore long ago, and has recovered, in one moment, all its old ties, its old feelings, its old friends, and pleasure! O that you were but here to see, and to share the delight of your affectionate son.

Chapter 2

The Years Between 1836-1849

Kingsley went up to Cambridge in 1838 as an undergraduate at Magdalene. He was a tall, thin, wiry youth with a prominent nose and jaw, and a thin but mobile mouth. He spoke with a slight West Country accent (which his wife was later to refer to as a 'twang') but, at the drop of a hat, would regale his friends with stories in broadest Devonshire. He smoked a workman's clay pipe ceaselessly and talked with equal vigour, although, according to one friend, much of what he said was 'the most awful rot'.

At Cambridge he fished the fen rivers, shot the fen duck, and hunted foxes across the flat countryside. He learnt to row and to box, but amidst all this excitement he did not lose interest in natural history. He followed Professor Sedgwick's mobile geological lectures on a hired hack and went on long bird-watching expeditions with his close friend, Charles Mansfield. He made up his mind to become a barrister—a fact unknown to his biographers that has only recently come to light. The following entry can be seen in the records of admissions to Lincoln's Inn: 'Charles Kingsley (Junior) Magdalene College Cambridge (19) son of Rev Charles Kingsley, Rector of Chelsea, admitted 3rd April 1839.'*

During his first summer vacation from Cambridge the most important event in Kingsley's life occurred: he met his future wife, Fanny. His father had exchanged duties with the rector at

* I am indebted to Thomas Shelford, Bencher of Lincoln's Inn, for his researches into the records of Lincoln's Inn.

Checkenden, near Ipsden in Oxfordshire, and it was on the lawn at Checkenden rectory that Charles first saw her. Frances Eliza Grenfell was the youngest of the twelve children of a Cornish tin magnate, Pascoe Grenfell. On her mother's side she was related to the St Legers, an aristocratic Devonshire family who owned property in Ireland. Fanny lived at Braziers Park with her sisters, a formidable group who had formed themselves into a kind of religious sisterhood of the kind recommended by Pusey and the high Anglicans. But Fanny was not quite like her sisters. She was not only younger and simpler than they were, but also prettier. Her portraits show a comfortably plump young woman with shining brown hair and beautiful eyes.

For Kingsley it was love at first sight; 'that was our true wedding day', he wrote in a letter years later. Fanny felt the same. 'How I remember your wild troubled look that first day, as if you lived such *lone* life, and I felt, from our first conversation, that I alone could understand you, that I alone had the key to your spiritual being and could raise you to your proper height.'

For the next five years the couple corresponded, and Charles's love letters, which have recently become available, must be some of the strangest ever written. The meeting with Fanny had made him conscious of his own impurity, and gradually he realised that the only way to rid himself of his guilt was to return to the Church and become a priest. Having made this resolution and having had his name taken off the books at Lincoln's Inn,* he settled down, in his final year at Cambridge, to do some belated studying. At the beginning of January 1842, to his surprise, he achieved a second class in mathematics and set about preparing for the classical examinations. By the middle of February, how-

---

* 'Council held on November 2nd, 1841. Five benchers present. Upon the petition of Charles Kingsley Esq. a Fellow of the Society, praying that his name be taken off the books, having given up his intention of being called to the Bar, the usual Order was made.' (Minutes of the meetings of the Benchers of Lincoln's Inn.) Kingsley's coat of arms can still be seen in the west window above the Bench table in the New Hall. It is included among those of other distinguished former members who made careers outside the law.

ever, his brains were in such a 'be-Greeked' state that he could study no more. 'I read myself ill this week, and have been ordered to shut up every book till the examination. The last three weeks have been spent in agonies of pain with leeches on my head,' he wrote. He was in a state of deep depression, and wrote to his mother, 'that degree hangs over me like a vast incubus keeping me down. I feel deeply what Manfred says of an order

> Of mortals on the earth, who do become
> Old in their youth, and die ere middle age.

I shall be an old man before I am forty.' He even expressed a wish to die.

In fact he gained a first class and immediately sought the balm of the West Country to apply to his throbbing head. Equipped with a fishing rod and a trunk full of books on theology, he went to Holne, the village where he had been born, but which he had never actually seen, to prepare for ordination. He invited Cowley Powles, an old school friend, to join him: 'I shall be most happy to have you as temporary sharer in the frugality of my farm house lodgings. Whether you will despise hard beds and dimity curtains, morning bathes and evening trout fishing, mountain mutton and Devonshire cream, I do not know, but you will not despise the chance of a few weeks in which to commune with God's works.'

We have disappointingly few records of that first stay on Dartmoor. No doubt the two young men strode from tor to tor, enjoying the gentle advance of spring across the face of the moor. No doubt they threw a rod over every stream they came across and brought home bags full of trout for their landlady to overfry. No doubt they were enthralled by the bird life, the plant life and the geology of that magnificent remnant of the primeval wilderness. But all that Kingsley put into his letters to Fanny was theology.

25

After his ordination Kingsley obtained a curacy at Eversley, then a remote village surrounded by heathland, within earshot of the drums of Aldershot. The rectory stood next to the church a mile from the village, but Kingsley was not permitted to live there. He had to content himself with a room in a cottage on the village green where he dreamed of the day when he could live in the rectory with Fanny for a wife. Her sisters were determined that she should not marry the uncouth curate from Hampshire and for two more weary years Kingsley had no alternative but to continue to pour his frustrated passion into endless love letters to her.

In order to reconcile his guilt about his urgent physical need of Fanny with his strict religious beliefs, he had concocted a theory about sex that was, to say the least, unusual. He became convinced that the sexual act was a sacrament, that he was the priest, Fanny the victim and the bed the altar. He designated Thursday nights 'Festival nights'. On Thursdays at ten he and Fanny, in their widely separated beds, lay in imagination in each other's arms, intoning the *Te Deum*. On Friday nights he lay naked on the floor and scourged himself. 'O how I long to kiss away those stripes,' Fanny confided to her diary. Charles made many drawings of his hallowed love-making and these also Fanny preserved in her diary.

At the end of 1843 the rector of Eversley committed an indiscretion 'of a most revolting nature' with a female member of his congregation and was obliged to flee the country. The living was left vacant and Sir John Cope, the patron, offered it to Kingsley. He accepted it with alacrity and within months was settled at the rectory with his beloved Fanny.

Kingsley was an enormously conscientious man. He was determined to be everything that a rector should. When he came to Eversley the parish had been shockingly neglected. There were sheep in the churchyard; not a single labouring person in the parish could read and few of them attended church. He now set to work to woo them back. He organised evening classes and confirmation classes; he went from cottage to cottage visiting (and often treating) the sick. What he saw in those cottages sickened him; whole families crammed into one leaky bedroom, open sewers before the door, no water supply within half a mile in many cases. Undismayed he set about organising a one-man welfare service, for these were the Hungry Forties when the only form of social security was the workhouse, and a labouring man was lucky to earn ten shillings a week. He ran a maternal society, a shoe club and a loan fund, and he pestered Sir John Cope continually, in his palace at Bramshill, about improvements.

In 1848 the clarion call of a larger section of the working class than that which lived at Eversley was heard. The Chartists took their petition for universal suffrage to Westminster and the streets of London were expected to run with blood. Full of excitement, Kingsley rushed up to town, eager to join in the fray; and with F. D. Maurice, the famous theologian, and Tom Hughes, author of *Tom Brown's Schooldays*, he became one of the first Christian Socialists and helped edit their periodical, *Politics for the People*.

But mental collapse was once more imminent, for Kingsley was exerting himself on too many fronts. Fanny was now the mother of two children, Rose and Maurice, and only the best was good enough for them. Eversley rectory, a spacious double-fronted seventeenth-century house, she now condemned as damp. She insisted on expensive alterations, and to pay for them Kingsley set about writing a serialised novel called *Yeast*. Because it dealt with the living conditions of the rural poor, he dared not put his name to it. He had to write it late at night, for his days were already fully occupied with his parish and with *Politics for the People*. He was also giving a weekly lecture on Early English Literature to the young ladies at Queen's College, a post that F. D. Maurice had procured for him.

Once more he longed to die, and one Sunday evening he fell

into a sleep so deep that it seemed very close to death. He woke only late the following day and was so exhausted that his doctor ordered him to Bournemouth where Fanny had relations. The month he spent there failed to lift his depression and in the end he insisted that the only cure for his disease would be a dose of the 'Far West'. And so, in January 1849, the whole Kingsley family moved to Ilfracombe for a prolonged stay.

Ilfracombe was already a miniature resort, but the fact that it never figured in any of Kingsley's books suggests that he felt no special affection for it. It was very much more Fanny's kind of place than his, for she revelled in fashionable watering places with marine parades. After a frantic 'nesting' session she discovered Runnamede Villa 'a perfect bijou of a place having everything that could be wished for except a view of the sea'.

Kingsley's condition was pitiable. He could not write; talking was an effort and, after an hour's reading, he said, 'My poor addle brain feels as if someone had stirred it with a spoon.' Even the exertion of walking or riding was beyond him. But he was a man who had always been extraordinarily sensitive to the influence of climate and landscape. His letters were full of references to the weather and its effect on his physical and mental condition; two of his most famous poems were addressed to the north-east and the south winds respectively. After a few days of brisk Atlantic breezes he wrote to his mother 'a tremendous gale of wind has acted on me exactly like champagne and Cathedral organs in one, and restored my, what you call nervous, and what I would call magnetic tone'. Kingsley was in fact being over-optimistic, for it was nearly a year before he completely recovered his health.

The days at Ilfracombe were sad ones. Kingsley had desperate money worries. From his salary as rector of Eversley he had to pay a curate to run the parish as well as the rent of the house at Ilfracombe. Furthermore, with two small children to care for, Fanny insisted on travelling with a considerable nursery staff. Gradually, however, Kingsley's strength returned and his daily walks became longer, 'although I get a strange swimming in the wits now and then, at seeing farm houses under my feet, and cows feeding like so many flies on a wall'. Eventually his doctor even gave him permission to mount a horse once more, and he rode a hireling over to Morte Sands, the huge beach a few miles west of Ilfracombe that was named after the Morte Stone (or death rock) always awash far out at sea. The day was a grey one and the horse a weary hack; Kingsley was painfully conscious of his affinity with the wretched beast. He once wrote, of that endless beach, 'What a place for a "gloom-pampered" man to sit and misanthropize', and in the set of elegiacs composed after that ride he did just this:

Wearily stretches the sand to the surge, and the surge to the
  cloudland;
Wearily onward I ride, watching the water alone . . .
No more on a magical steed borne free through the regions of
  ether,
But, like the hack which I ride, selling my sinew for gold.
Fruit-bearing autumn is gone; let the sad quiet winter hang o'er me—
What were the spring to a soul laden with sorrow and shame?
Blossoms would fret me with beauty; my heart has no time to
  bepraise them;
Gray rock, bough, surge, cloud, waken no yearning within.
Sing not, thou sky-lark above! even angels pass hushed by the
  weeper.
Scream on, ye sea-fowl! my heart echoes your desolate cry.
Sweep the dry sand on, thou wild wind, to drift o'er the shell and
  the sea-weed;
Sea-weed and shell, like my dreams, swept down the pitiless tide.
Just is the wave which uptore us; 'tis Nature's own law which
  condemns us;
Woe to the weak who, in pride, build on the faith of the sand!
Joy to the oak of the mountain;* he trusts to the might of the rock
  clefts;
Deeply he mines, and in peace feeds on the wealth of the stone.

* The 'oak of the mountain' referred to was F. D. Maurice.

It was perhaps the depression induced by that ride on Morte Sands that in April led Kingsley to move his family along the coast to Lynmouth. It is not known which house the Kingsleys rented in that enchanted village where the river cuts a deep wooded cleft in the cliffs to reach the sea. Certainly he must have found the little place far more to his liking than Ilfracombe, yet it too was never to figure in any of his works.

Kingsley was now well enough to indulge his boyhood passion for natural history once more. He spent many happy hours collecting specimens on the seashore. Triumphant letters were written to his parents about the successful bottling of 'a comatula with his legs by great dodging', and plaintive ones about the disappearance of one of his boyhood favourites, the Venus Maidenhair. 'Where, oh where,' he cried, 'is the Venus Maidenhair gone? I have hunted every wet rock shute. Pray inform me.' It was while the Kingsleys were staying at Lynmouth that they invited the disgraced young fellow of Exeter College, Oxford, J. A. Froude, to be their guest, and there the future historian met his wife, Fanny's sister Charlotte Grenfell.

By June, Kingsley thought he was strong enough to return to Eversley. At this stage in his life he was undoubtedly a manic depressive; moods of high euphoria alternated with ones of deep melancholia. He was now entering once more upon a manic phase. He rushed up to London, eager to join ranks with his fellow Christian Socialists against the forces of repression and cruelty. As a result of his book, *Yeast*, he was beginning to be known. He called on Thomas Carlyle (who was to become a close friend) and Francis Newman (an Anglican theologian, brother of the cardinal). He was invited to breakfast with the Prussian Ambassador, Baron de Bunsen. Back at Eversley he was equally busy. Many of his parishioners were suffering from a low fever that was expected to flare up into cholera and there were not enough nurses to go round. Kingsley himself insisted on helping to care for the sick. Fanny tells us that after a night sitting up with a labourer's wife, the mother of a large family, giving her the nourishment every half hour on which her life depended, he broke down completely. After only two months, euphoria had turned once more to depression.

Chapter 3

The Return to Clovelly 1849

Once more Kingsley longed to lay down his clerical burden and escape to the West Country. But this time he longed for something else as well—to be away from Fanny. Deeply though the Kingsleys loved each other, their temperaments were growing increasingly different; the romantic, religious Fanny of the love letters was turning into a bustling, practical, organising woman who was too often tempted to scold her impractical, unbusinesslike husband for his unworldliness. Fanny was aware of this failing in herself: 'I chafe you with my Martha-ism and efforts after Order, you chafe me with little unpunctualities and then comes the Wall and we must shout to hear each other.'

For relief from the shouting, Kingsley sought the calm of Clovelly, a place where he could cease to be a clergyman or even a husband and become a boy again. A German psychologist once interpreted Kingsley's love of the West Country as a desire to return to the womb; through an inadequate knowledge of English, he had read 'Wet Country' for 'West Country', but he was nevertheless not so far off the mark.

Kingsley was obsessed with the idea of washing and water. This obsession can be explained by his deep-seated feeling of guilt about sex. He adored Fanny but he could not rid himself of the feeling that he was sullied by sexual relations with her. In his letters he was constantly entreating her to kiss herself all over *in the bath* for him. This obsession helps to explain the recurrent image in his writing of women near, or in, water: the lady who sat by Trehill Well in his earliest poem; Rose Salterne wading out naked into the sea in *Westward Ho!*; Andromeda bathed all night by the sea spray in the epic poem of that name. His preoccupation with water is, of course, most clearly demonstrated in *The Water-Babies*, the story of the dirty little chimney sweep who comes down clean little Ella's chimney. To atone for his filth, Tom must become a water-baby, be washed for ever more in a pure, submarine world. It was surely the closeness of North Devon to this pure, submarine world that made it so dear to him.

Kingsley travelled westward by sea. At Appledore, on 10 August 1849, he had time to write home to Fanny:

Here I am, no boat having come from Clovelly, to which place a trawler has engaged to take me nine miles for 5s tomorrow morning at eight. A delicious passage down, in which I fell in with a character, a Cornish shipowner . . . who has insisted on my drinking tea with him this evening, and on my coming to see him in September at Boscastle, near Padstow, where he will give me sailing in his little yacht, and take me to seal caves, where they lie by dozens. He is, of course, like all Cornishmen, a great admirer of your father. Strange, what a name your father seems to have made for himself. The man is a thorough Cornishman: shrewd, witty, religious, well informed, a great admirer of scenery; talks about light, and shadow, and colouring more like an artist than a brown fisted merchant skipper, with a mass of brain that might have made anything had he taken to books. I feel myself already much better. The rich, hot, balmy air, which comes in now through the open window off Braunton Burrows, and the beautiful tide river, a mile wide, is like an Elixir of life to me.

Appledore was a village that always held great charm for Kingsley. Situated downstream from Bideford, at the confluence of the estuaries of the rivers Torridge and Taw, overlooking Braunton Burrows, it had been a flourishing little port since Elizabethan times, being the first place within Bideford Bar where ships could lie up. Ship-building had been one of Apple-

C   33

dore's chief industries for four hundred years. Its streets were still narrow Elizabethan ones, known locally as 'drangs', and many of the white Georgian houses on the quay had studio-like windows on the upper floors intended to illuminate sail-lofts.

Kingsley was a passionately keen sailor. For him, the last part of the journey to Clovelly, in a bucketing little trawler, was infinitely preferable to the first part in a coastal steamer reeking of oil and cattle. Sailing brought him closest to his beloved element, water—'the wonderful ocean world! Three-fifths of our planet!'—and it provided the 'animal excitement' he craved. On this occasion he had to wait for some time for the 'animal excitement', for the boat was becalmed: 'And now we are on board; and alas! some time before the breeze will be so. Take care of that huge boom, swaying and sweeping backwards and forwards across the deck, unless you wish to be knocked overboard. Take care, too, of that loose rope's end, unless you wish to have your eyes cut out. Look at those spars, how they creak and groan with every heave of the long glassy swell. How those sails flap and thunder with rage, only because they are idle.' At last the wind was heard approaching. 'Louder and nearer swells "the voice of many waters" . . . till the air strikes us; and heels us over; and leaping, plunging, thrashing our bows into the seas, we spring away close-hauled. Exquisite motion! More maddening than the crash of the thorn hedges before the stalwart hunter, or the swaying of the fir-boughs in the gale, when we used to climb as schoolboys after the lofty hawk's nest!'*

As the little boat scudded along, he strained his eyes for a sight of Clovelly and saw 'in the long straight wall of cliffs which bounded the broad bay . . . a faint perpendicular line of white houses'. As the distance decreased, 'the rock clefts grew sharper and sharper before us. The soft mass of the lofty bank of wooded cliff rose higher and higher. The white houses of Clovelly, piled stair above stair up the rocks, gleamed more and more brightly

* Charles Kingsley, *Prose Idylls*.

out of the green round bosom of the forest. As we shut in headland after headland, one tall conical rock after another darkened with its black pyramid the bright orb of the setting sun. Soon we began to hear the soft murmur of the snowy surf line; then the merry voices of the children along the shore; and running straight for the cliff foot, we slipped into the little pier from whence the red-sailed herring-boats were swarming forth like bees out of a hive full of gay handsome faces, and all the busy blue-jacketed life of seaport towns, to their night's fishing in the bay.'

It was the custom in that happy place, as he once pointed out, for every woman, young or old, to kiss 'a young fellow just landed from a foreign voyage', as he came 'rolling up the street'. Whether Kingsley was accorded this welcome we do not know, but certainly it was a joyful homecoming. 'I felt a new life, renewing my youth like the eagle's the day after I got here. The very smell is a fragrance from the fairy gardens of childhood,' he wrote to his mother. He added, 'this place seems *more* beautiful than of old. Contrary to one's usual experience in visiting old scenes, the hills are higher, the vegetation more luxurious, the colouring richer than I had fancied.'

The fisherfolk of Clovelly had not forgotten him or his family. On his first night there were parties in almost every one of the little white-washed houses down the street, to greet him. 'I was in and out of all the houses last night, like a ferret in a rabbit burrow—all so kind.' He took a room with Mr Whitefield,* a fisherman, and wrote home to Fanny to describe it. 'My room is about 12 ft square on the first floor, a jessamine, and a fuchsia running up to the windows. In front, two or three small houses, above which, and right in front, towers the wall of wood, oak, ash and larch as tender and green as if it were May and not August. I am near the top of the street. On the left, that is down the hill, I see, from my windows, piled below me, the tops of the

* There are still Whitefields in the area.

nearest houses, and the narrow paved cranny of a street, vanishing downwards stair below stair, and then above all, up in the sky it seems, from the great height at which I am, the glorious blue bay, with its red and purple cliffs. The Sand-Bar, and Braunton, the hills towards Ilfracombe, and Exmoor like a great black wall above all. The bay is now curling and writhing in white horses under a smoking south-wester, which promises a blessing, as it will drive the mackerel off the Welsh shore where they now are in countless millions, into our bay; and then for fun and food for me and the poor fellows here, who are at their wits end, because some old noodles of doctors have persuaded people that fish gives the cholera.'

Not every Victorian clergyman could have settled down so happily to live with simple working people. Kingsley, like the hero of his novel *Yeast*, 'suffered from a continual longing to chat with his inferiors'. Fanny, in her biography, tells us that he was never at a loss for a subject of conversation with either a huntsman or a poacher 'for he knew every fox cover on the moor and every pike hover and chub hole' in the local waters. And with fishermen he was even more at ease, for he secretly preferred seamen to landsmen. He once pointed out that the notorious wreckers who lived by plundering stranded ships came always from the inland farms. The fishermen, on the contrary, would risk their lives in small boats to save the shipwrecked crews.

He was fascinated by the character of his landlord, Mr Whitefield, 'whose delicate and gentlemanlike features and figure were strangely at variance with the history of his life,—daring smuggler, daring man-of-war sailor, and then most daring and successful of coastguard-men. After years of fighting and shipwreck and creeping for kegs of brandy . . . he had come back with a little fortune of prize money to be a village oracle.' Another close friend was 'Old Wimble', a fisherman who had known him since he was a boy. 'Old Wim potters in, like an old grey-headed Newfoundland dog about three times a day to look after me in all sorts of kind and unnecessary ways,' Charles told Fanny. He was besieged with gifts of fish and offers of free boat rides. Soon after his arrival he attempted to repay some of the hospitality he had received: 'Last night I gave a tea-party with cream and your cake, which is too good for me, to my landlady and Mr and Mrs Wimble and we all agreed we only wanted you and my mother: as it was we were very merry, and finished with prayers.'

In spite of the elation produced by his return to Clovelly, Kingsley was still far from well. For the first few days he seldom left his room. 'I am as stupid as a porpoise,' he wrote to a friend. 'I lie in the window, and smoke and watch the glorious cloud phantasmagoria, infinite in colour and form, crawling across the vast bay and deep woods below, and draw little sketches of figures, and do not even dream, much less think.' The 'little sketches' to which he refers were more of the type that Fanny had preserved in her diary. They represented her and Charles making allegorical love and she now found them highly embarrassing. To Charles they were an outlet for the frustration of being deprived of her physically.

Eventually Kingsley felt strong enough to walk with a friend through Sir James Hamlyn Williams's famous Deer Park on the cliff tops west of Clovelly, that 'little strip of paradise between two great waste worlds of sea and moor'. The walk was well documented because, before the year was out, he contributed a lengthy account of his holiday, entitled 'North Devon', to *Fraser's Magazine*, a periodical owned by his Christian Socialist friend, John Parker the printer:

> I question whether anything ever charmed me more than did the return to the sounds of nature which greeted me to-day, as I turned back from the dreary, silent moorland turnpike into this new road terraced along the cliffs and woods . . . and listened to a glorious concert in four parts, blending and supporting each other in exquisite harmony, from the shrill treble of a thousand birds, and the soft

melancholy alto of the moaning woods, downward through the rich
tenor hum of innumerable insects who hung like sparks of fire beneath
the glades of oak, to the bass of the unseen surge below . . .

As we wandered along the edge of the cliff, beneath us on our left
lay lawns spotted with deer . . . Glens of forest wound away into the
high inner land . . . while from the lawns beneath, the ground sloped
rapidly upwards towards us, to stop short in a sheer wall of cliff, over
which the deer were leaning to crop the shoots of ivy, where the slipping of a stone would have sent them 400 feet perpendicular into the sea.

Kingsley was in fact describing the approaches to Gallantry
Bower, a headland that he always insisted, no doubt with little
historical evidence, was so called because of 'the gay Norman
squire who . . . kept his fair lady in the old watch tower, on the
highest point of the White Cliff—now a mere ring of turf
covered stones'. From this vantage point he was amazed, as
generations of travellers have been, by the view of Bideford Bay:

Beneath, the sea was shrouded in soft summer haze. The far Atlantic
lay like an ocean of white wool, out of which the Hartland Cliffs and
the highest point of Lundy just showed their black peaks. Suddenly as
we stood watching, a breeze from the eastward swept the clouds out,
packed them together, rolled them over each other, and hurled them
into the air miles high in one Cordillera of snowy mountains, sailing
slowly out into the Atlantic; and behold, instead of the chaos of mist,
the whole amphitheatre of cliffs, with their gay green woods and spots
of bright red marl and cold black ironstone, and the gleaming white
sands of Braunton, and the hills of Exmoor bathed in sunshine, so near
and clear we almost fancied we could see the pink heather hue upon
them.

Down we wandered from our height through the deep glades of the
park towards the delicious little cove which bounds it. A deep crack
in the wooded hills, an old mill half-buried in rocks and flowers, a
stream tinkling on from one rock-basin, to another towards the beach,
a sandy lawn gay with sea-side flowers over which wild boys and bare-
footed girls were driving their ponies with panniers full of sand, and as
they rattled back to the beach for a fresh load standing upright on the
backs of their steeds, with one foot in each pannier, at full trot over
rocks and stones where a landsman would find it difficult to walk on
his own legs.

The cove Kingsley was describing was Mouth Mill, a place that always aroused the geologist in him, for there the layers of ancient rock—buried deep underground in most parts of England—stand up high in almost perpendicular strata. 'What extraordinary rocks! How different from those Cyclopean blocks and walls along the Exmoor cliffs are these rich purple and olive ironstone layers, with their sharp serrated lines and polished slabs, set up on edge, snapped, bent double, twisted into serpentine curves, every sheet of cliff scored with sharp parallel lines at some fresh fantastic angle. Yes; there must have been strange work here when all these strata were being pressed and squeezed together like a ream of wet paper between the rival granite pincers of Dartmoor and Lundy.'

Another more ambitious walk took Kingsley right over the Hartland peninsula, to Tonacombe, just inside the Cornish border. Tonacombe Manor, a fine medieval house standing high on the cliffs, was in the parish of Morwenstow, and although Morwenstow was at that time described as 'a wretched hamlet',* its rector was the poet-priest Robert Stephen Hawker, author of *And shall Trelawny Die?* The two men had known each other since Kingsley was a young man and although he had always spoken kindly of Hawker, Hawker was almost invariably unkind about Kingsley. He dubbed him 'nosey' and, of the great controversy that later occurred between Kingsley and Newman, remarked acidly, 'I should think the contest must be unequal.'

Hawker was one of the great eccentrics of the last century. The son of a Plymouth doctor, he had, as a boy, dressed himself in seaweed and sat on a rock at Bude combing his long hair; a farmer took a shot at him but missed. Halfway through his career at Oxford he heard that his father could no longer support him, so he immediately proposed marriage to a lady twice his age, who had 'taught him his letters', and was accepted. As

* John Murray, *Guide to Devon*, 1851.

rector of Morwenstow, Hawker continued eccentric both in his dress and his behaviour. His habitual outfit, when visiting his parishioners, was a long-tailed claret-coloured coat with a yellow poncho over it, a blue fisherman's sweater with a cross on one side to mark the place where Our Lord was speared, high sea-boots and a beaver hat. If he entered a cottage where he knew there was an unbaptised child he would sniff the air loudly and say: 'I smell brimstone.'

During 1849 Kingsley saw a good deal of this strange man, probably because there were very few other people in the area with whom he could hold a cultivated conversation. The views of the two men differed on many points, and Kingsley would no doubt have been horrified to hear that Hawker became a Roman Catholic on his death-bed. Nevertheless the poet-priests took many walks together and on several occasions visited the strange little hut that Hawker had tunnelled into the headland known as Vicarage Cliff. The hut was made from timber salvaged from the *Alonzo*, one of the many wrecks along that coast. In it Hawker wrote many of his poems and vituperative letters. As the two men sat side by side at the back of the hut, they could see nothing but a great wall of water. If they walked out to the end of the headland they could see a line of dwindling headlands stretching in both directions. Magnificent Marsland Mouth, with its solitary cottage, was only a couple of miles to the north. Two miles to the south was the site of the old house of the Grenvilles at Stowe, which the two men visited on a famous occasion recorded by Hawker.*

With returning health came the urge for more manly activities, and one fine August morning Kingsley set off westwards from Clovelly with a pony and a fishing rod to fish the Torridge, high up on the moors, at the West Country Inn. He described those moors as 'a desolate table-land of rushy pastures and mouldering banks' and regretted that they were not farmed.

* C. S. Byles, *The Life & Letters of the Rev. R. S. Hawker, 1803–1875* (1905).

'The only cultivators here, and through thousands of acres of the North of Devon, are the rook and the mole: and yet the land is rich enough... There are scores of farms of far worse land in Mid-England, under a four-course shift, yielding their load of wheat an acre ... and the shrewd Cornishmen of Launceston and Bodmin have awakened long ago to the new gospel of fertility. When will North Devon awake?' As he brushed through the heather on his long-tailed pony he answered his own rhetorical question. The word 'Damnonii' meant 'dwellers in the valley', he mused, and if you asked a typical member of the tribe why he only cultivated the low land he would reply, 'Vather did zo, and gramfer did zo, and why shouldn't Jan do the zame?'

The sight of the boisterous mountain river at this point put him into a more cheerful frame of mind. It was 'just clearing from last night's showers. A long transparent amber shallow, dimpled with floating silver rings by rising trout; a low cascade of green-veined snow; a deep dark pool of swirling orange-brown, walled in with heathery rocks, and paved with sandstone slabs and boulders, distorted by the changing refractions of the eddies —a sight delicious to the angler.'

After two hours of happy fishing, however, a storm of rain came in from the Atlantic. 'Down it came. The brown hills vanishing in white sheets of hail, first falling perpendicularly, then slanting and driving furiously before the cold blast which issued from the storm.' Man and beast sheltered as best they could on the lee side of a small rise. 'The rock above us rang with the thunder peels, and lightning, which might have fallen miles away, seemed to our dazzled eyes to dive into the glittering river at our feet.' After half an hour of this he decided to make for Clovelly and shelter. He set off at a canter, with the rain cutting his face 'like showers of pebbles'. The little mountain pony, its long mane and tail 'streaming out wildly' in the wind, could barely keep its feet at times, and 'more than once was . . . blown sheer up against the bank by some mad gust'. He consoled himself for

41

such discomforts by amazing the fishermen of Clovelly with the trout he had caught: 'among them one of 2 lbs!!! Never was such a trout seen in Clovelly before.'

A trip to Lundy organised by Mr and Mrs Whitefield, in a cutter, was the high point of the stay at Clovelly:

It was four o'clock on an August morning. Our little party had made the sleeping streets ring with jests and greetings, as it collected on the pier. Some dozen young men and women, sons and daughters of the wealthier coasting captains and owners of fishing-smacks . . . As soon as all had settled themselves comfortably on board, and the cutter was slipping quietly away under the magnificent Deer Park cliffs, the Lady Abbess, pulling out her Wesleyan hymn-book, gave out the Morning Hymn, apparently as a matter of course.

With hardly a demur, one sweet voice after another arose; then a man gained courage, and chimed in with a full harmonious bass: then a rich sad alto made itself heard, as it wandered in and out between the voices of the men and women; and at last a wild mellow tenor, which we discovered, after much searching, to proceed from the most unlikely-looking lips of an old dry, weather-bleared, mummified chrysalis of a man, who stood aft, steering with his legs, and showing no sign of life except when he slowly and solemnly filled his nose with snuff.

We had landed, and laughed, and scrambled, eaten and drunk, seen all the sights of Lundy, and heard all the traditions. Are they not written in Mr Bamfield's *Ilfracombe Guide*? . . . But neither pirate legends, nor tales of cheated insurance officers nor wrecks and murders, will make us understand Lundy. It may be defined as a lighthouse-bearing island. The whole three miles of granite table-land, seals, sea-birds, and human beings, are mere accidents and appendages—the pedestal and the ornament of that great white tower in the centre, whose sleepless fiery eye blinks all night over the night-mists of the Atlantic. If, as a wise man has said, the days will come when our degenerate posterity will fall down and worship rusty locomotives and fossil electric-telegraphs, the relics of their ancestors' science, grown to them mythic and impossible, as the Easter-islanders bow before the colossal statues, left by a nobler and extinct race, then surely there will be pilgrimages to Lundy, and prayers to that white granite tower, with its unglazed Lantern and rusting machinery, to light itself up again and help poor human beings.

After shooting a red-legged chough or two, and one of the real black English rats—ousted on the mainland by the grey Hanoverians—the party settled down to meditate on the high western cliffs of Lundy. In his slightly fictionalised account Kingsley puts certain of his meditations into the mouth of an imaginary artist, Claude Mellot, who in fact represented another side of himself, a side that he did not feel entirely suited to the clerical life. Claude admitted to 'strange longings' as he gazed out 'yonder over the infinite calm' towards America, the new world, the great Titan-baby. 'Oh that I had wings as a dove, then would I flee away and be at rest! Here, lead me away; my body is growing as dizzy as my mind. I feel coming over me that horrible longing of which I have heard, to leap out into empty space. How the blank air whispers, "Be free!" How the broad sea smiles, and calls, with its ten thousand waves, "Be free!" As I live, if you do not take me away I shall throw myself over the cliff!'

Kingsley made no mention, in this account, of the magnificent seabirds to be seen from those western cliffs of Lundy, but he remedied the omission some years later in *Madame How and Lady Why*, a book explaining geology to children. 'Oh, what a screaming and what a fighting! What are those beautiful little ones, like great white sea swallows with crested heads and forked tails, who hover, and then dip down and pick up something? They are terns. And there are gulls in thousands, you see, large and small, grey-backed and black-backed; and over them all two or three great gannets swooping round and round...'

When the time came to leave Lundy, they set off homeward in the red-sailed cutter. 'The cliff-wall of Lundy stood out blacker and blacker every moment against the gay western sky; greens, greys, and purples, dyeing together into one deep rich monotone ... Before us the blue sea and the blue land-line were fading into mournful grey on which one huge West Indiaman blazed out, orange and scarlet, her crowded canvas all a-flame. A few moments and she too had vanished into the grey twilight, and a chill night-wind crisped the sea . . .'

Chapter 4

Northdown Hall, Bideford 1854-1855

Kingsley ended his rest cure in Devonshire by walking across Dartmoor from north to south. Once more on the crest of the wave, he returned home to tackle the problem of cholera in London, and particularly in a foul area of Bermondsey known as Jacob's Island, where the only available drinking water came from a canal slimy with sewage. He sought interviews with the prime minister and with Lord Carlisle, and succeeded in obtaining one at Oxford with Bishop Samuel Wilberforce. He insisted that a public meeting be called as soon as possible and, in the meantime, set about organising a water supply for Jacob's Island single-handed, or rather with the aid of his faithful Christian Socialist colleagues, Charles Mansfield and John Ludlow.

Kingsley's second novel, *Alton Locke*, was the direct outcome of this campaign. It purported to be the autobiography of a cockney poet, and it did for the London working class what *Yeast* had done for the farm labourers. In one of its most lurid scenes Jem Downes, a destitute tailor, overcome by the sight of his wife and children lying dead on the floor of a hovel on Jacob's Island, throws himself into the sewer behind it. 'The light of the policeman's lantern glared over . . . the black waters . . . over bubbles of poisonous gas, and bloated carcasses of dogs and lumps of offal, floating in the stagnant olive green hell-broth, over the slow sullen rows of oily ripples . . . the only sign that a spark of humanity, after years of foul life, had quenched itself at last in that foul death.'

Passages such as this aroused the public conscience, but they also aroused public hostility. In the part of the book that described Alton Locke's visit to Cambridge, Kingsley came very near to attacking the Establishment. Meanwhile he continued to be an active journalist in the cause of Christian Socialism. The periodical *Politics for the People* had petered out, but in 1850 its editors produced the first issue of its successor, *The Christian Socialist*. A year later *Yeast* appeared for the first time in book form (it was originally issued as a serial).

Kingsley was invited to preach at St John's Church, Charlotte Street, on 'The Message of the Church to Labouring Men'. The sermon was one in a series in honour of the Great Exhibition and the occasion was a memorable one. Kingsley's homily, though mild enough, contained a reference to a law of Moses that forbade the accumulation of large estates. The vicar of St John's took this to be an attack on the landed classes and, when Kingsley had ceased speaking, rose to declare that he considered what the preacher had just said was dangerous and untrue. The church was in an uproar. The working men who were present crowded round Kingsley with cries of 'God bless you, sir!' and he kept silent only with difficulty.

All that night he paced his study at Eversley, unable to sleep. As so often in times of personal crisis, Kingsley reverted to the images of his boyhood to echo his distress, and it was during that night that he wrote *The Three Fishers*, a poem about shipwrecked fishermen, which has been set to music several times.

> Three fishers went sailing away to the West,
>   Away to the West as the sun went down;
> Each thought on the woman who loved him the best,
>   And the children stood watching them out of the town;
>   For men must work, and women must weep,
>   And there's little to earn, and many to keep,
>   Though the harbour bar be moaning.

Three wives sat up in the lighthouse tower,*
And they trimmed the lamps as the sun went down;
They looked at the squall, and they looked at the shower,
And the night-rack came rolling up ragged and brown.
But men must work, and women must weep,
Though storms be sudden, and waters deep,
And the harbour bar be moaning.

Three corpses lay out on the shining sands
In the morning gleam as the tide went down,
And the women are weeping and wringing their hands
For those who will never come home to the town;
For men must work, and women must weep,
And the sooner it's over, the sooner to sleep;
And good-bye to the bar and its moaning.

The following morning he was the object of a massed attack from the newspapers, who described him as 'The Apostle of Socialism'. Worse still, he received a letter from the Bishop of London forbidding him to preach in any London church. Once the bishop had actually read the sermon he withdrew his embargo, but the damage was done, and there were many in the hierarchy of the Church of England who never again fully trusted Kingsley.

Had the bishops taken the trouble to read Kingsley's two Christian Socialist novels, they would have discovered that his socialism was of a very mild variety. The moral of *Alton Locke*, he explained to a critic, 'is that the working man who tries to desert his class and rise above it, enters into a lie'. He considered the upper class was the one best fitted to rule, but that it lacked a sense of responsibility to the workers. The workers, meanwhile, should improve their own lot by education and co-operation, and not attempt to take over the government of the country.

Kingsley always considered himself a member of that upper class. 'Ours is an old but landless family,' he had proudly de-

* Kingsley was referring to the Braunton lighthouse on the north bank of the Taw-Torridge estuary, two miles upstream from Bideford bar.

clared to Fanny before they married. He was often embarrassed by the company of his immediate social inferiors. With the true working man, particularly the countryman, he was always at ease, but he found the town lower middle class—'the cockneys', as he called them—hard to stomach. At meetings of the Promoters of Association in London he often had to sit with what Tom Hughes described as 'bearded men, vegetarians and other eccentric persons'. On one of these occasions he was 'quite upset and silenced by the appearance of a member in a straw hat and blue plush gloves. He did not recover from the depression induced by those gloves for days.'*

Now a more serious depression was on the way, aggravated no doubt by money worries. Fanny's attempts to maintain the standards to which she was accustomed ran her husband into constant debt; in the course of the past two years he had been obliged to borrow £1,000 and take a private pupil, John Martineau (who later became a friend and admirer). By July 1851 it was obvious that, regardless of expense, he must have another of his holidays away from Fanny. This time the Rhineland, and not the West Country, was chosen, and Charles went in the company of his parents and his brother Henry.

Kingsley's behaviour in the Eiffel Mountains was very similar to his behaviour on the Devon moors. In the company of Henry he walked twenty miles a day, filling his socks with rocks to take home to his daughter, Rose (who at six was a keen geologist). His letters crackled with pressed flowers for Fanny (who was probably not as keen a botanist as he would have wished). The two brothers were dressed so eccentrically that on one occasion they were arrested and spent a night in the gaol at Trier as suspected Mazzini spies. Kingsley never dressed like a clergyman even in his parish. At Eversley he was often taken for a farmer. But for the German holiday he affected the near fancy dress of a wide-brimmed 'Mazzini' hat.

* Tom Hughes, preface to *Alton Locke*.

(*above*) Clovelly seen from the Hobby Drive

(*below left*) Delivering coal in Clovelly Street

(*below right*) Clovelly Rectory

(left) Clovelly church

(right) Tonacombe,
Morwenstow

The holiday was a great success but Kingsley found that 'abroad' lacked the essential characteristic of Devonshire, a certain bracing purity. Germany was *too* charming and, if one stayed there long, one might be tempted to subside into a life of hedonistic idleness. To Fanny he wrote, 'I understand now, at once, why people prefer this to England. It *is* a more charming country, and that is the best of reasons one has for thanking God that one has not the means of escaping to it.' He was both fascinated and repelled by the 'pagan luxury' of Europe. Above all, the Roman ruins mesmerised him. In the amphitheatre at Trier he felt he was standing over the skeleton of 'the giant iniquity, Old Rome', and he imagined 'the hellish scenes of agony and cruelty' that the place had witnessed, when droves of Frankish prisoners were put to death there.

It was under this inspiration that he went home to start work on his first historical novel, *Hypatia*, the story of a beautiful female philosopher who lectured on Neoplatonism in Alexandria. The book was published in 1853 and met with a mixed reception. The royal family was rumoured to have enjoyed it, but Lewis Carroll thought the crude portraits of early Christian monks 'outrageous to taste', and Tennyson said he 'really was hurt' that Hypatia had to appear 'naked', before being hacked to death with oyster shells. Kingsley was by now something of a celebrity, even if a notorious one. When in town he dined with many of the great literary men of his day, and a distinguished Swedish novelist, Frederika Bremer, who had come over for the Great Exhibition, declared she would rather see the author of *Alton Locke* than the Crystal Palace.

Yet all was not well at Eversley. Fanny complained constantly of the damp at the rectory and often suffered from 'the influenza'. After a difficult pregnancy she had given birth to Kingsley's second daughter Mary (eventually to become a famous novelist under the name of Lucas Mallet), but she was slow in rallying from this, her third confinement. In the autumn of 1853 she had a bad miscarriage, and a persistent cough was giving cause for concern. She also became convinced she was suffering from a heart complaint, and that it was dangerous for her to leave her sofa. She decided that the family must leave Eversley for a prolonged period.

The fact that fashionable Torquay was chosen as their place of retreat proves that, although Charles was approaching one of his periodic collapses, on this occasion at least, it was Fanny's health that was the cause of the move westwards. London carriages and foreign aristocrats thronged the streets of the resort and a section of the best London society spent a period of each year there. Kingsley once described the way these people spent their days. 'A great deal of dressing, a lounge in the club-room, a stare out of the window with the telescope, an attempt to make a bad sketch, a walk up one parade and down another, interminable reading of the silliest of novels, over which you fall asleep on a bench in the sun, and probably have your umbrella stolen; a purposeless fine weather sail in a yacht, accompanied by many ineffectual attempts to catch a mackerel, and the consumption of many cigars; while your boys deafen your ears, and endanger your personal safety by blazing away at innocent gulls and willocks, who go off to die slowly . . . And after all, and worst of all, at night a soulless *réchauffé* of third-rate London frivolity.'* Kingsley soon had an added reason for disliking Torquay. Not long after his arrival the Bishop of Exeter declared that all pulpits in the town were closed to the author of *Yeast*, *Alton Locke* and *Hypatia*.

In the summer of 1854, the Kingsleys moved from the fashionable south coast of Devon to the still undiscovered north coast. Charles chose to settle in the little port of Bideford on the Torridge estuary because he was already planning a second historical novel, this time to be set in the age of Elizabeth and to deal with the adventures of the great sea captains of the West. He was no

* Charles Kingsley, *Glaucus*.

doubt influenced in his choice of Bideford by the fact that it lay only a few miles east of his beloved Clovelly, on the same bay.

Bideford was, then as now, the prettiest town in North Devon. It stood on the west bank of the Torridge at a point where the river widened towards its estuary, and where it could, at low tide, be forded. The most striking feature of the town was its bridge, built of oak on wool bales in 1300, and clad in stone in 1460. Because the original timber lintels were of different lengths, the twenty-four stone arches varied in width from 12ft to 25ft. From the bridge a view could be obtained downstream of the broad shining estuary as far as Appledore, and upstream to the dark woods of Annery. Bideford itself presented a charming spectacle, climbing up the side of an emerald green hill. Its main street, which ran along the riverside quay, had delighted travellers since the days of Defoe and before. Architecturally of greater interest still was Bridgeland Street, running at right angles to the river, up the steep hillside. It was laid out by Nathaniel Gascoyne around 1690 and was flanked by spacious merchants' houses, for it was in the late seventeenth century that Bideford prosperity, based on the tobacco trade with Virginia, had been at its peak.

From 1760 onwards the fortunes of Bideford had declined as a result of the American War of Independence. By the time Kingsley arrived, however, there was a temporary revival of activity down on the quay. A brisk traffic in emigrants to America had developed and four first-class boats were sailing regularly. The town was prospering, its population increasing and there was employment for many in the breweries, the lime kilns and the potteries. Bideford earthenware, made from the local clays of Fremington and Peters Marsland, was famous.

In 1854 Kingsley was able to travel as far as Barnstaple by train, for the famous engineer, Thomas Brassey, had just laid the broad-gauge line from Crediton and was, the following year, to extend it to Bideford. Kingsley had been a passionate convert

to railway travel ever since its introduction ten years earlier. 'Great railroads and the great railroad age!' he once apostrophised. 'Who would exchange you, with all your sins, for any other time?' He declared that even the 'exquisite motion' of a Clovelly trawler under sail was not 'so maddening as the new motion of our age—the rush of the express train, when the live iron pants and leaps and roars through the long . . . cuttings'.*
In North Devon the cuttings themselves were of immense interest to him geologically, for they revealed the ancient rock strata of the West Country tipped on end. He commented on the phenomenon in *Madam How and Lady Why*: 'See how all the way along the railroad the new rocks and soils lie above the older, and yet how, when we get westward, the oldest rocks rise highest into the air.'

There is a tradition that on arrival at Bideford Kingsley stayed for a time at the Royal Hotel,† East-the-Water, on the far side of the bridge. If he did, he displayed taste, for the house had been built by John Davies, a merchant, in 1688 and, in an upper room, boasted one of the finest plaster ceilings in North Devon, with a wreath executed in the most daring relief, some of the flowers being almost completely detached from their background. By midsummer, however, the entire Kingsley family had arrived and were established at Northdown Hall, the property of a local landowner, Captain George Molesworth, RN. Northdown Hall stood back from the Strand, formerly the shoreline of the Pill, a tributary of the Torridge.

Fanny must have set her heart on the house, for there is a letter in existence in which the fact that Kingsley had rented it was announced to her in letters half-an-inch high followed by three exclamation marks.‡ He might well feel the news de-

---

* Charles Kingsley, *North Devon*.
† It seems unlikely, since the Royal was a workhouse before 1872. However, the hotel receptionist claims that, since the publication of *The Beast and the Monk*, Kingsley's ghost has begun to walk.
‡ Unpublished letter to Fanny, No 135, 1855.

manded such emphasis, for Northdown Hall was enormous. Fanny could no longer be satisfied with 'perfect little bijoux' of places. It was a cube-shaped house of the last years of the eighteenth century; the ground floor comprised an entrance hall embellished by a fine curved staircase that appeared to float down without visible means of support, and two reception rooms which, with their interconnecting door open, were large enough for a private ball. From the window of the upstairs corner room where he wrote, Kingsley had a view over the park-like walled garden and, beyond it, to the shipyards.

Life had evidently not been entirely peaceful at Torquay. There is a rather pathetic passage in another letter of Kingsley's written at this time: 'My dear Fanny! I cannot help looking forward to a twelvemonth with you at Northdown as a blessed time. How happy we may be, and shall be, please God, this summer together.' He hoped that at Northdown he could enjoy the uninterrupted company of his family, while Fanny continued to benefit from the mild western climate, 'where the flowers of Autumn meet the flowers of Spring'.*

In fact, as so often happens on these occasions, he quickly tired of the exclusively feminine company in which he found himself, for his household consisted of nurses and nursemaids, and a governess who did her best to oblige by searching for specimens on the seashore. 'I am utterly without male companions,' he complained in a letter to F. D. Maurice. This was not entirely true, for he did in fact make one very good male friend in Bideford, and that was Dr W. H. Ackland.

Dr Ackland was a man after Kingsley's own heart. Although he was a member of one of Devonshire's oldest aristocratic families and lived in a fine, double-fronted, bow-windowed house at the top of Bridgeland Street, he was also deeply concerned for the welfare of the working classes, and particularly concerned with the state of their drains. While Kingsley was living at

* Charles Kingsley, *Glaucus*.

Bideford there was an outbreak of cholera in the town and Dr Ackland persuaded him to take a district for house-to-house visitation. More agreeable visitations were the ones that the two men made to patients around the countryside, or to Lundy Island in a storm-tossed fishing boat to visit an emergency case. It became the doctor's custom to stop his horse at the corner of Northdown Hall and signal to Kingsley who would leap from his desk to join him. It was probably with Dr Ackland that Kingsley first visited the Braunton Downs beyond Barnstaple, from which he could see the green and red patchwork of the Devon countryside stop abruptly like a table hundreds of feet above the Atlantic. He announced it was the finest view in the kingdom. On another drive with Ackland, when the two men were on their way to Woolsery for a day's fishing, the clergyman confided to the doctor that he had spent the previous Thursday on the west coast of Lundy. 'I sat down opposite Shutter Rock, and took it all in, and yesterday I wrote it all out. When I got home I said to my wife, "My trip, my dear, has cost me half-a-guinea, but I have put five-and-twenty pounds in my pocket, for I have got a whole chapter for *Westward Ho!*".' Later Kingsley became godfather to Ackland's son, who was called Charles Kingsley after him. He presented him with a set of sermons on his second birthday and recommended his father to 'feed him on cream and commend him to God'.

Another male companion was an old friend from Helston school days, who was a big landowner in the area, but Kingsley probably preferred the right to shoot his woodcock to his conversation, and found more entertainment in the company of the young artisans of the town for whom he organised a drawing class. Mr Plucknett, one of the young men who attended these classes, wrote a description of them many years later to Kingsley's widow:

I was a youth in Bideford at the time Mr Kingsley came to reside there, when seeing the young men of the town hanging about wasting their leisure hours in worse than wasting, his heart yearned to do them good. He at first endeavoured to establish a Government School of Art—this, however, failed. He then offered to teach a class drawing, gratuitously. A few of us held a meeting, and hired a room in the house of the Poet Postman, Edward Capern, who, although a married man, much older than the rest of us, was a most hard working pupil. I look back upon those evenings at Bideford as the pleasantest part of my life, and, with God's blessing, I attribute my success in life to the valuable instruction I received from Mr Kingsley: his patience, perseverance, and kindness won all hearts and not one of his class but would have given his life for the master. He used, as no doubt you remember, to bring fresh flowers from his conservatory for us to copy as we became sufficiently advanced to do so; and still further on he gave us lectures on anatomy, illustrating the subject with chalk drawings on a large black board. His knowledge of geometry, perspective, and free hand drawing, was wonderful; and the rapid and beautiful manner in which he drew excited both our admiration and our ambition. I have reason to believe that most of the class received lasting benefit, and have turned out well. Personally, I may say, with truth, I have cause to bless the name of Mr Kingsley as long as I live; for I left home with little more than the knowledge of my business, and the knowledge of drawing learned in the class. After many years of hard work I am now at the head of a good business, which I am proud to say is well known for the production of art furniture.

When the class came to an end, Kingsley invited all its members to Northdown Hall. At the end of 'a happy evening' they presented him with a silver card case, which he treasured for the rest of his life.

The poet postman, Edward Capern, in whose house in Mill Street the classes were held, was known to many literary men besides Kingsley. He possessed letters from Tennyson, Froude, Longfellow, Dickens and Lord Palmerston. Walter Savage Landor had declared that some of his 'noble verses' were equal to 'the best of Burns'. Capern composed most of his poetry while on his round between Bideford and Buckland Brewer, four miles to the south. In William Widgery's portrait of him at Bideford he is portrayed as a sturdy looking character wearing a tam-o'-

shanter and a plaid muffler. His postbag is slung over his
shoulder and in his left hand he holds a couple of letters, in his
right a pen. In real life the right hand would have held the bell
with which he used to announce his arrival, and which was to be
attached to his tombstone.

While Kingsley was at Bideford he sometimes took services at
churches in the surrounding villages. He did occasional duty at
the great church at Hartland, and also at Abbotsham. He preached
several times from the pulpit at St Margaret's, Northam. Northam church stood on the edge of a cliff overlooking the sea, and
its tall pinnacled tower was visible for miles around. The font
was thirteenth century, but the spacious north aisle had been
added at the end of the sixteenth, as was proclaimed in the
inscription; 'This yele was made anno 1593.' The monuments
which must have particularly interested Kingsley were those of
the Leigh family. He would also have noted the oval inscription
plate with ornate black-letter script that commemorated Sir
Charles Chalmers, who had been a big local landowner when
Kingsley's father was rector of Clovelly.

The church where the Kingsley family attended divine service
more regularly was St Mary's, Bideford. At that time it was a
largely fourteenth-century church with a plain unpinnacled
tower and a remarkable Norman font where, it was always
claimed, the first Indian brought from the New World, a man
called Ralegh, had been baptised, only to die a year later. The
church was remarkable for a tower screen made from Devon's
famous bench ends, many of them carved with the Grenville
arms. There were other memorials to the Grenville family in
the form of tombs going back over the centuries; one of the
finest was that of Sir Thomas Graynfyldd, who died in 1513.
He lay, carved in stone on a tomb chest, under a finely carved
stone canopy. There were also mural monuments to the Bideford
merchants, who had made the city rich in the seventeenth and
eighteenth centuries.

During the year in Devonshire, Kingsley, who was thirty-five, rediscovered his boyhood passion for 'conchologising'. Now, however, his interest went beyond shells and included all the creatures to be found along the shore-line. In the last few years Philip Gosse, the naturalist, had, with his books on shore-life and home aquaria, encouraged young ladies to plunder the coastal rockpools. Kingsley, who started a correspondence with Gosse—and even became his friend until he found the Plymouth Brother too hard to stomach—had joined eagerly in the hunt. During the winter in Torquay he had despatched hampers full of specimens to Gosse; he had even discovered three entirely new species, besides a number of Montague's Chirodata which had not been seen since the lynx-eyed Colonel George Montague discovered them in a cave at Goodrington forty years earlier.

At Bideford, Kingsley continued his search for sea beasts, although he had fewer hours to devote to it, being at work on a novel. Rose and Maurice Kingsley, aged ten and eight respectively, were now a sturdy pair and shared eagerly in their father's hobby. Indeed it was probably their pleasure that revived Kingsley's own interest, for he was, all his life, immensely fond of children. His pleasure in wandering among rocks and pools was greatly enhanced by 'the laugh of children drinking in health from every breeze and instruction in every step, running ever and anon with proud delight to add their little treasure to their father's stock'. At Northdown Hall delightful evenings were spent 'over the microscope and the vase, in examining, arranging, preserving and noting down in the diary the wonders and the labours of the happy, busy day'.

Eventually Kingsley published his letters to Gosse in the form of a lengthy article for the *North British Review*, and this in turn he expanded into a book, published towards the end of 1855 under the title of *Glaucus** or *The Wonders of the Shore*. The

---

* Glaucus, as classical scholars will know, was a mythical Greek fisherman who learned to live under the sea.

book was intended to persuade English schoolboys that the study of nature was a manly, even chivalrous pursuit. In this it failed, if one is to judge by Stalky & Co who declared 'bug-huntin's a filthy business', when at school near Northam beach twenty years later.*

Glaucus has bequeathed a vivid picture of the adventures of the Kingsley family down by the water. One of their favourite hunting grounds was that very Northam despised by Kipling's schoolboy heroes, for it was the nearest point on the Atlantic coast from Northdown Hall. The great charm of Northam was the famous pebble ridge which kept the sea from washing over the thousand acres of marshy grazing known as Northam Burrows. The ridge was composed of boulders traditionally considered to have broken off Hartland Point and been rolled round Bideford Bay by the tide to their present position. (A certain Clovelly fisherman used to swear that a boulder with an iron spike in it that he had seen on the shore at Clovelly eventually turned up at Northam.) It was the duty of the potwallopers of Northam and Appledore, who had the right to graze cattle and geese on the Burrows, to throw pebbles up on to the ridge once a year in order to mend breaches in it. The Kingsleys, however, were more concerned with the marine life that could be found there in abundance.

There were also treasures to be found underneath the boulders of the pebble ridge at low tide when the sea had dropped far below the stones, leaving the famous beach exposed. Kingsley used to employ 'a strong-backed quarry man with a strong-backed crowbar, as is to be hoped (for he snapped one right across yesterday falling miserably on his back into a pool thereby) . . .' In *Glaucus* he described what was found under the rock: 'Now the crowbar is well under it, and so, after five minutes' tugging, propping, slipping, and splashing, the boulder gradually

---

* Kipling was at the United Services College, Westward Ho!, from 1878 to 1882.

tips over, and we rush greedily upon the spoil. A muddy dripping surface it is, truly, full of cracks and hollows, uninviting enough at first sight: let us look it round leisurely, to see if there are not materials enough for an hour's lecture. The first object which strikes the eye is a group of milk-white slugs, from two to six inches long, cuddling snugly together.' The learned father then proceeded to identify for the benefit of his children 30 different molluscs, 40 annelids, 5 crustacea, 5 echinoderns and 24 polyps.

For more ambitious expeditions Kingsley would take the children to the river in his sailing boat, the *Curlew*,* and drop down slowly with the tide till the wide waterway became wider with the coming of the Taw. As he glided past Appledore he could hear the ring of the shipbuilder's mallet and see the smoke from fires heating pitch for caulking. As he rounded the pebble ridge, its great stones groaning and murmuring under the Atlantic swell, the ocean burst into sight. The spire of Northam church high on its bluff was clearly visible, rising above the Burrows, a well-known bearing point for sailors crossing the dangerous bar. The Kingsleys' destination was usually one of the beaches near Clovelly where the falling tide would have deposited a wealth of miniature monsters.

> . . . What a variety of forms and colours are there, amid the purple and olive wreaths of wrack, and bladder-weed, and tangle (oarweed as they call it in the south), and the delicate green ribbons of the Zostera (the only English flowering plant which grows beneath the sea). What are they all? What are the long white razors? What those tiny babies' heads, covered with grey prickles instead of hair? The great red star fish, which Ulster children call 'the bad man's hands'; and the great whelks, which the youth of Musselburgh know as roaring buckies . . .
>
> Next, what are the striped pears? They are sea anemones, and of a species only lately well known, *SagartiaViduata* . . . Here, adhering to this large whelk, is another, but far larger and coarser. It is *Sagartia*

* For years after Kingsley left Bideford, the *Curlew* was treasured with almost religious fervour.

Parasitica, one of our largest British species; and most singular in this, that it is almost always found adhering to a whelk: but never to a live one; for this reason. The live whelk burrows in the sand in chase of hapless bivalve shells . . . Now, if the anemone stuck to him it would be carried under the sand daily, to its own disgust. It prefers, therefore, the dead whelk, inhabited by a soldier crab, of which you may find a dozen anywhere as the tide goes out; and travels about at the crab's expense, sharing with him the offal which is his food. Note, moreover, that the soldier crab is the most hasty and blundering of marine animals, as active as a monkey, and as subject to panics as a horse; wherefore the poor anemone on his back must have a hard life of it; being knocked about against rocks and shells, without warning, from morn to night, and night to morn. Against which danger kind Nature ever has provided by fitting him with a stout leather coat.*

To collect specimens from underneath the sea Kingsley preferred to hire a small trawler from Clovelly, where so many of the fishermen were personal friends. 'Dredging,' he declared, 'is an amusement in which ladies, if they will, may share, and which will increase, and not interfere with the amusements of a water-party. The naturalist's dredge should differ from the common oyster-dredge in being smaller: certainly not more than four feet across the mouth; and instead of having but one iron scraping lip like the oyster-dredge, it should have two, one above and one below, so that it will work equally well on whichsoever side it falls. The bag-net should be of strong spun yarn, or (still better) those hides of wild cattle of the Pampas, which the tobacconists receive from South America, cut into thongs, and netted close . . . The dragging rope should be at least three times as long as the perpendicular depth of the water in which you are working.'

At Clovelly, in the summer of 1854, Kingsley discovered a new species in his bag-net. It was a type of sea anemone rediscovered and named *Sagartia Venusta* two years later by Gosse. Kingsley found it on oyster-lumps in deep water and had in-

* Charles Kingsley, *Glaucus*.

tended to despatch it to the Plymouth Brother, but the creature perished in an aquarium left on a sunny window-sill at Northdown Hall.

That summer the British public was in the grip of the fever of hate for the Tsar Nicholas I that precipitated the Crimean War. Kingsley was as filled with blood lust as anyone. He longed for 'an hour's skirmishing in those Inkerman ravines and five minutes with butt and bayonet as a *bonne bouche* to finish off with'. Tom Hughes suggested he should express himself in a nationalistic ballad, but he replied, 'as for a ballad—oh! I tell you the whole thing stuns me, so I cannot sit down to make *fiddle* rhyme with *diddle* about it, or *blundered* with *hundred*, like Alfred Tennyson. *He* is no Tyrtaeus, though he has a glimpse of what Tyrtaeus ought to be. But I have not even that; and am going rabbit shooting tomorrow instead. Would that the Rabbits were Russians, tin pot on head and musket in hand!' And so he put his aggression into a novel—*Westward Ho!*—in which it was understood that the public was to read 'Russian' where it saw 'Spaniard' or 'Jesuit'.

A letter to F. D. Maurice of 19 October gives a vivid picture of his state of mind while he was writing the book: 'I am shut up like any Jeremiah here, living on the newspapers and my old Elizabethan books. The novel is more than half done, and a most ruthless bloodthirsty book it is (just what the times want, I think) . . . I am afraid I have a little of the wolf-vein in me, in spite of fifteen centuries of civilisation . . . Sooner one caress from a mastiff than twenty from a spaniel . . . This war would have made me half mad, if I had let it. It seemed so dreadful to hear of those Alma heights being taken and not be there; but God knows best, and I suppose I am not fit for such brave work; but only like Camille Desmoulins, *"une pauvre créature, née pour faire des vers"*. But I can fight with my pen still (I don't mean in controversy—I am sick of that. If one went on at it, it would make one a very Billingsgate fishwife, screaming and scolding, when one knows one is safe, and then running away when one expects to have one's attack returned).—Not in controversy, but in writing books which will make others fight. This one is called *Westward Ho!*'

While he was writing it, Kingsley was kept afloat financially by his publisher, Daniel Macmillan. Letters preserved by the Macmillan family enable us to follow the progress of the book. In one of the most interesting of these, dated 11 November 1854, Kingsley calculated that 400 pages were already with the publisher, 250 more were nearly ready to go, and 300 remained to be written. He apologised for the fact that the book, when completed, would be 950 pages long, which was more than he had promised, but explained that he would prefer not to cut it. He added, however, that he was quite willing to either shorten or lengthen the novel by one-third if required. In a typically absent-minded postscript he added, 'Did I enclose "How Eustace met the Pope's Legate"? *Please return at once.*' Macmillan's reply is not preserved, so we shall never know whether the sixteen-page chapter describing the adventures of Amyas Leigh in Ireland had to be rewritten.

By December, *Westward Ho!* was finished and Kingsley had achieved the amazing feat of writing a book of a quarter of a million words,* and doing the research for it, in just over six months. The book's success was instant and colossal. It became a best-seller overnight and by 1897 had been reprinted thirty-eight times. Even the Royal Academy did not escape the impact of the legend, and one of its 1890 successes was a painting depicting Cary's duel with Don Guzman, named 'On Bideford Sands'.

Westward Ho! brought Kingsley fame, money and, most important, acceptance in elevated social circles. The Queen showed her approval by appointing him her chaplain and from then on he was assured of a niche in the establishment. He became

* *Westward Ho!* was originally published in three volumes.

Regius Professor of History at Cambridge and, when he died in 1876 at the age of fifty-six, he was a canon at Westminster Abbey.

His success brought to an end his perpetual nervous breakdowns and, with them, the need for regular doses of the West Country. Thereafter his summer holidays were spent salmon fishing at the houses of the great in Scotland and Ireland. He never ceased to regard Clovelly as his true home, however. During his nine years at Cambridge he often amused, and sometimes shocked, his fellow dons with stories told in broad Devonshire about the country folk of Clovelly. Three years after he left the beloved county, he named his youngest son, Grenville, in its honour and books and poems about Devonshire still came from his pen.

Posterity has never been able to decide whether or not Kingsley was a poet. It was a point on which he himself was very uncertain. In 1855, after *Andromeda*, an epic, had not met with success, he confided to the Rev R. H. Gurney: 'I have deserted poetry as rats do a sinking ship. I have refused to publish my poems, actually ashamed of being called a poet, of being caught out in such a bad company (not yours, of course), and have taken to monosyllabic prose, as the highest achievement of man; considering modern taste so radically rotten, that I must unlearn almost all I have learnt from it and recommence with my alphabet and Mrs Trimmer. I can tell more truths in prose than I can in verse, and earn ten times as much money, wherefore Parnassus has been my retreat, I doubt not, with dry eyes!' However, in 1858, encouraged by the publication of his poems in book form, he declared 'poems are, after all, what I can do best'.

The truth probably lies somewhere between the two pronouncements. The long poems were often marred by a tendency to preach. 'As a parson to the British public,' he explained to his friend Ludlow, 'I am *expected* to point a moral.' In his shorter poems and ballads there was no room for sermons, and it was this fact combined with a freshness of expression and a galloping rhythm, that caused them to last and in some cases to become almost as familiar to the British public as the old nursery rhymes. Many people, for instance, imagine that the line 'For men must work and women must weep' is a traditional saying, and are quite unaware that it came from the best poem Kingsley ever wrote about Devonshire.

Kingsley continued to correspond with Dr Ackland for many years and a letter written to him in 1861 (on display in Bideford Library) describes Kingsley's feelings on hearing of the death of Sir James Hamlyn Williams. 'Poor old Sir James! I did not know he had suffered so much as you say. His death is another link with the past and the West Country broken. I am afraid my lot in life will not take me thither again—and yet I love it better than all the world beside and should like to crawl back thither to die, when my work is done.'

Kingsley did in fact go there once more, towards the end of his life, for the purpose of delivering the presidential address to the Devonshire Association in 1871. The lecture was mostly about natural science, but it included an opening paragraph or two of personal reminiscences about Devonshire, that beloved corner where Nature can be seen at 'her purest and noblest'. He was relieved to find that the only observable change was the widening of Bideford Bridge. 'With a sigh of relief I find still unabolished the Torridge and the Hubbastone, and Tapeley and Instow and the Bar and the Burrows and the beloved old Braunton marshes and sandhills.'

Kingsley's last sight of the western peninsula was in the final year of his life. He was returning by sea from a lecture tour of America and, although he left no description of it, it must have looked much as it did when he saw it four years earlier, on his way back from the West Indies. 'Land's End was visible, and as we neared the Lizard we could see not only the lighthouse on the

(above) Hartland Point
lighthouse

(right) Hartland church

Clovelly harbour and the Red Lion

cliff, and every well known cave and rock from Mullion and Kynance round to St. Keverene, but far inland likewise.'

At Christmas 1875 Fanny took to her bed with angina and was pronounced to be dying (although she in fact lived for another fourteen years). Unable to bear the thought of parting from her, Charles, who was far from well himself, sat by her bedside for three weeks, reliving old memories and reading aloud favourite poems. It was a bitter winter at Eversley and the bedroom windows had to be kept open for Fanny to get her breath. Inevitably Charles contracted pneumonia.

For many days the couple lay in separate bedrooms at opposite ends of Eversley rectory, able to communicate only by pencilled notes. Once, unable to resist the temptation, Charles made the journey through the icy bedrooms that separated him from Fanny, and sat by her bed. 'Don't speak,' he said. 'This is heaven!' But soon a fit of coughing came on and he could say no more. On 20 January a severe haemorrhage started. 'Heynes!' he cried to his physician, 'I am hit! This last shot has told.' He asked if Fanny knew and, on being told, 'She knows all,' assumed that she had gone to heaven to await him. Content, he lapsed into a coma. On the night of the 22nd he was heard repeating the burial service aloud. He died at noon the following day.

Chapter 5

'Westward Ho!'

If Kingsley had written no other book or poem, *Westward Ho!* alone would have earned him the title of North Devon's leading writer. Although the book's main characters were Elizabethan seamen who were away much of the time slaughtering Spaniards in South America and elsewhere, nevertheless many of its 600 pages were devoted to minute and loving descriptions of the North Devon coast, which have never been bettered. Not the least of these is the one of Bideford (or Bidevor as the country people called it) with which the book opens.

All who have travelled through the delicious scenery of North Devon must needs know the little white town of Bideford which slopes upwards from its broad tide river paved with yellow sand and many-arched old bridge where salmon wait for Autumn floods, toward the pleasant upland on the west. Above the town the hills close in, cushioned with deep oak woods, through which juts here and there a crag of fern fringed slate; below they lower, and open more and more in softly rounded knolls, and fertile squares of red and green, till they sink into the wide expanse of hazy flats, rich salt marshes, and rolling sand hills, where Torridge joins her sister Taw, and both together flow quietly toward the broad surges of the bar and the everlasting thunder of the long Atlantic swell. Pleasantly the old town stands there, beneath its soft Italian sky, fanned day and night by the fresh ocean breeze, which forbids alike the keen winter frosts, and the fierce thunder heats of the midlands; and pleasantly it has stood there for now, perhaps, eight hundred years.

The hero of the book, Sir Amyas Leigh, Knight, of Burrough,

in the county of Devon, was a lusty, flaxen-haired lad, brave as a lion cub but with little use for book learning. At the beginning of the book, in 1575, he was still a schoolboy at Bideford Grammar School, hanging about the many taverns on the quay, hoping to overhear yarns from the men who had 'picked the lock of the New World'. Like them he believed that 'one west countryman can fight two easterlings, and an easterling can beat three Dons any day'. It was on such an occasion that he saw the swaggering Captain Oxenham and his lieutenant, the gaunt Anabaptist Salvation Yeo recruiting men with the aid of a marvellously carved buffalo horn. The horn was in fact a map of the Spanish Main. 'See here boys, all and behold,' declared Yeo, in the broad Devonshire of a Clovelly man, 'the pictur of the place, dra'ed out so natural as ever was life . . . Take mun over, and I'll warrant you'll know the way in five minutes so well as ever a shark in the seas.'

The horn filled young Amyas's head with dreams of adventure, and as he walked home to Northam, the proud possessor of the horn, he resolved to take ship for the west as soon as he was able.

So he goes up between the rich lane—banks, heavy with drooping ferns and honey suckle; out upon the windy down toward the old Court, nestled amid its ring of wind-clipt oaks; through the grey gateway into the homeclose; and then he pauses a moment to look around; first at the wide bay to the westward, with its southern wall of purple cliffs; then at the dim Isle of Lundy far away at sea; then at the cliffs and downs of Morte and Braunton, right in front of him; then at the vast yellow sheet of rolling sand hill, and green alluvial plain dotted with red cattle, at his feet, through which the silver estuary winds onward towards the sea. Beneath him, on his right, the Torridge, like a land locked lake, sleeps broad and bright between the old park of Tapeley and the charmed rock of the Hubbastone, where, seven hundred years ago, the Norse rovers landed to lay siege to Kenwith Castle, a mile away on his left hand; and not three fields away, are the old stones of 'The Bloody Corner', where the retreating Danes, cut off from their ships, made their last fruitless stand against the Saxon

71

sheriff and the valiant men of Devon.* Within that charmed rock, so Torridge boatmen tell, sleeps now the old Norse Viking in his leaden coffin, with all his fairy treasure and his crown of gold; and as the boy looks at the spot, he fancies and almost hopes that the day may come when he shall have to do his duty against the invader as boldly as the men of Devon did then. And past him, far below, upon the soft south eastern breeze, the stately ships go sliding out to sea. When shall he sail in them, and see the wonders of the deep?

In two years' time the lad had his way. His father being dead, his godfather, the great Sir Richard Grenvil,† who owned a fine house in Bideford and another just over the Cornish border at Stowe, decided the time had come for the boy to go to sea. A berth was forthwith found for him on Sir Francis Drake's *Pelican*.

The next set piece in the book described the scene at St Mary's Church, Bideford, when Amyas and four companions returned three years later, after circumnavigating the world:

It is nine of the clock on a still, bright November morning; but the bells of Bideford church are still ringing for the daily service two hours after the usual time; and instead of going soberly according to wont, cannot help breaking forth every five minutes into a jocund peal, and a very flower garden of all the colours, swarming with seamen and burghers, and burghers' wives and daughters, all in their holiday attire. Garlands are hung across the streets, and tapestries from every window. The ships in the pool are dressed in all their flags, and give tumultuous vent to their feelings by peals of ordnance of every size. Every stable is crammed with horses; and Sir Richard Grenvil's house is like a very tavern, with eating and drinking, and unsaddling, and running to and fro of grooms and serving men. Along the little churchyard, packed full with women, streams all the gentle blood of North Devon, —tall and stately men, and fair ladies, worthy of the days when the gentry of England were by due right the leaders of the people by personal prowess and beauty, as well as by intellect and education. And

* Modern historians claim that Kenwith Castle is a medieval earthwork, and that the defeat of the Danes in 878 took place at Countisbury, the ancient Arx Cynuit.
† Kingsley preferred to use the archaic spelling of Grenville.

first, there is my lady Countess of Bath, whom Sir Richard Grenvil is escorting cap in hand . . . and there are Bassets from beautiful Umberleigh, and Carys from more beautiful Clovelly, and Fortescues of Wear, and Fortescues of Buckland, and Fortescues from all quarters, and Coles from Slade, and Stukelys from Affton, and St Legers from Annery and Coffins from Portledge and even Coplestones from Eggersford, thirty miles away: and last, but not least (for almost all stop to give them place), Sir John Chichester of Ralegh, followed in single file, after the good old patriarchal fashion, by his eight daughters, and three of his famous sons.

The service ended with a magnificent rendering of the *Te Deum*. 'And no sooner had the clerk given out the first verse of that great hymn, than it was taken up by five hundred voices within the church, in bass and tenor, treble and alto (for everyone could sing in those days, and the west country folk, as now, were fuller than any of music), the chaunt was caught up by the crowd outside, and rang away over roof and river, up to the woods of Annery, and down to the marshes of the Taw, in wave on wave of harmony. And as it died away, the shipping in the river made answer with their thunder, and the crowd streamed out again toward the Bridge Head, whither Sir Richard Grenvil, and Sir John Chichester, and Mr. Salterne, the Mayor,* led the five heroes of the day to await the pageant which had been prepared in honour of them.'

A fair lady who was missing from the celebrations was the daughter of the mayor, beautiful Rose Salterne. Because half the gallants of the county were in love with her, her father had banished her to her uncle's 'little farm house beside the mill, buried in the green depths of the Valley of Coombe halfway between Stow and Moorwenstowe'. But even here she was not safe from the attentions of her suitors, for Amyas's sly cousin Eustace lived close by in a house called Chapel, 'a great rambling, dark house' where priests were hidden in a turret and mass was

---

* The first mayor of Bideford was a John Salterne (Watkins, *History of Bideford*, 1792).

celebrated in a secret chamber in the roof. Eustace was not only a Roman Catholic vowed to the priesthood, but plotting for a 'rising of the West' which, coinciding with a similar one in Ireland, would overthrow Queen Elizabeth. On the occasion of his meeting with Rose he was accompanied by one of the plotters, Father Campian himself, travelling in disguise. 'They had just got to the top of the hill between Chapel and Stow mill, when up the lane came none other than Mistress Rose Salterne herself, in all the glories of a new scarlet hood, from under which her large dark languid eyes gleamed soft lightnings through poor Eustace's heart and marrow. Up to them she tripped on delicate ankles and tiny feet, tall, lithe, and graceful, a true West Country lass; and as she passed them with a pretty blush and courtesy, even Campian looked back at the fair innocent creature, whose long dark curls, after the then country fashion, rolled down from beneath the hood below her waist, entangling the soul of Eustace Leigh within their glossy nets.'

Rumours of Eustace's plots were reaching his cousins, Amyas and Frank Leigh. Frank was an exquisite, poetic creature, much favoured at court, 'as delicately beautiful as his brother was huge and strong'. But he was a gallant supporter of the Queen and the True Religion. What he saw one day, when visiting 'the little white fishing village' of Appledore with Amyas, increased his fears for the safety of the throne. Opposite the little 'Mariner's Rest' Inn four horses, loaded with saddles and mail bags, were being mounted by three gentlemen, one of whom was Eustace Leigh. It was the clumsy manner in which Eustace's two companions mounted their horses that revealed them for what they were . . . The strangers were, in fact, none other than the Jesuit plotters, Father Parsons and Father Campian. Discovering that they were on their way to Chapel, Eustace Leigh's house at Morwenstow, the Leigh brothers contrived to hunt a deer across the path of the two unskilled horsemen, who were 'ambling steadily and cautiously along the high tableland, towards Moor-

wenstowe* in the west . . .' Just as they came opposite Clovelly
Dykes, the huge old Roman encampment which stands about
mid-way in their journey, they heard a halloo from the valley
below, answered by a fainter one far ahead. At which, like a
couple of rogues (as indeed they were), Father Campian and
Father Parsons looked at each other, and then both stared round
at the wild, desolate, open pasture (for the country was then all
unenclosed), and the great dark furze grown banks above their
heads; and Campian remarked gently to Parsons, that this was
a very dreary spot, and likely enough for robbers.

'And as he spoke four or five more mounted gallants plunged
in and out of the great dykes, and thundered on behind the
party; whose horses, quite understanding what game was up,
burst into full gallop, neighing and squealing; and in another
minute the hapless Jesuits were hurling along over moor and
moss after a "hart of grease".'

Among the five gallants was young Will Cary whose father, a
regular hunting squire, was at that moment quaffing sack in the
'long, dark, wainscoted hall' at Clovelly Court. Young Cary of
Clovelly mightily enjoyed the sight of the hapless Father
Parsons 'in agonies of fear lest those precious saddlebags in front
of him should break from their lashings and, rolling to the earth,
expose such a cargo of bulls, dispensations, secret correspondence, seditious tracts, and so forth, that at the very thought of
their being seen, his head felt loose upon his shoulders'.

It was only after several miles of galloping that the Jesuits
were able to turn their horses' heads southwards over Bursdon
moor, leaving the hunters to crash 'down the Hartland glens
through the oak scrub and the great crown ferns' to Hartland
Abbey where their stag took to the sea.

Not long afterwards news reached Will Cary that an Irishman

---

* As a result of the historical researches of the Rev R. S. Hawker, the spelling
of Moorwenstowe was changed to Morwenstow. The village was named after
St Morwenna.

was going to land at Clovelly with a message for the Jesuits. Amyas and Frank were for watching the beach and the mill house at Mouth Mill, beyond the Deer Park, but Cary swore no boat could land there with a west wind blowing. He opted for a beach to the east of Clovelly called Freshwater, 'where the waterfall comes over the cliff, half a mile from the town. There is a path there up into the forest . . . Freshwater is as lonely as the Bermudas; and they can beach a boat up under the cliff at all tides, and in all weather except north and north-west.'

Cary proved right, as the brothers Amyas and Frank Leigh were to discover by moonlight that night:

So forth the two went, along the park to the eastward, and past the head of the little wood embosomed fishing town, a steep stair of houses clinging to the cliff far below them, the bright slate roofs and white walls glittering in the moonlight; and on some half mile farther, along the steep hill side, fenced with oak wood down to the water's edge, by a narrow forest path, to a point where two glens meet and pour their streamlets over a cascade some hundred feet in height into the sea below. By the side of this waterfall a narrow path climbs upward from the beach; and here it was that the two brothers expected to meet the messenger.

Frank insisted on taking his station below Amyas. He said that he was certain that Eustace himself would make his appearance, and that he was more fit than Amyas to bring him to reason by parley; that if Amyas would keep watch some twenty yards above, the escape of the messenger would be impossible. Moreover, he was the elder brother, and the post of honour was his right. So Amyas . . . obeyed him, after making him promise that if more than one man came up the path, he would let them pass before he challenged, so that both might bring them to bay at the same time . . .

Amyas took his station under a high marl bank, and bedded in luxuriant crown ferns, kept his eye steadily on Frank, who sat down on a little knoll of rock (where is now a garden on the cliff edge) . . . There Amyas sat a full half hour, and glanced at whiles from Frank to look upon the scene around. Outside, the south-west wind blew fresh and strong, and the moonlight danced upon a thousand crests of foam; but within the black jagged point which sheltered the town, the sea did but heave, in long oily swells of rolling silver, onward into the black shadow of the hills, within which the town and pier lay invisible, save where a twinkling light gave token of some lonely fisher's wife, watching the weary night through for the boat which would return with dawn . . .

At last he heard a rustle of the fallen leaves; he shrank closer and closer into the darkness of the bank. Then swift light steps—not down the path, from above, but upward, from below: his heart beat quick and loud. And in another half minute a man came in sight, within three yards of Frank's hiding place.

Frank sprang out instantly. Amyas saw his bright blade in the clear October moonlight.

'Stand in the queen's name!'

The man drew a pistol from under his cloak, and fired full in his face. Had it happened in these days of detonators, Frank's chance had been small; but to get a ponderous wheel lock under weigh was a longer business, and before the fizzing of the flint had ceased, Frank had struck up the pistol with his rapier, and it exploded harmlessly over his head. The man instantly dashed the weapon in his face and closed.

The blow, luckily, did not take effect on that delicate forehead, but struck him on the shoulder: nevertheless, Frank, who with all his grace and agility was as fragile as a lily, and a very bubble of the earth, staggered, and lost his guard, and before he could recover himself, Amyas saw a dagger gleam, and one, two, three blows fiercely repeated.

Mad with fury, he was with them in an instant. They were scuffling together so closely in the shade that he was afraid to use his sword point; but with the hilt he dealt a single blow full on the ruffian's cheek. It was enough; with a hideous shriek, the fellow rolled over at his feet, and Amyas set his right foot on him, in act to run him through.

'Stop! stay!' almost screamed Frank; 'It is Eustace! our cousin Eustace!' and he leant against a tree.

The message that Eustace was carrying declared that 800 Spanish troops had landed in Ireland. His cousins, having secured it, pursued him across the Hartland Peninsula in a memorable moonlight chase.

As they went over Bursdon, Amyas pulled up suddenly.

'Did you not hear a horse's step on our left?'

'On our left—coming up from Welsford moor? Impossible at this time of night. It must have been a stag, or a sownder of wild swine: or may be only an old cow.'

'It was the ring of iron, friend. Let us stand and watch.'

Bursdon and Welsford were then, as now, a rolling range of dreary moors, unbroken by tor or tree, or anything save few and far between a world-old furze-bank which marked the common rights of some distant cattle farm, and crossed then, not as now, by a decent road, but by a rough confused trackway, the remnant of an old Roman road from Clovelly dykes to Launceston. To the left it trended down towards a lower range of moors, which form the water-shed of the heads of Torridge; and thither the two young men peered down over the expanse of bog and furze, which glittered for miles beneath the moon, one sheet of frosted silver, in the heavy autumn dew.

'If any of Eustace's party are trying to get home from Freshwater, they might save a couple of miles by coming across Welsford instead of going by the main track, as we have done.' So said Amyas, who though (luckily for him) no 'genius', was cunning as a fox in all matters of tactic and practice . . .

'If any of his party are mad, they'll try it, and be stogged till the day of judgment. There are bogs in the bottom twenty feet deep. Plague on the fellow, whoever he is, he has dodged us! Look there!'

It was too true. The unknown horseman had evidently dismounted below, and led his horse up on the other side of a long furze-dyke; till coming to the point where it turned away again from his intended course, he appeared against the sky, in the act of leading his nag over a gap.

'Ride like the wind!' and both youths galloped across furze and heather at him; but ere they were within a hundred yards of him, he had leapt again on his horse, and was away far ahead.

Eustace Leigh's next adventure took place against the romantic backdrop of Marsland Mouth on the western side of the Hartland Peninsula. Nobody has described that coastline better than Kingsley himself at this point in *Westward Ho!*

And even such are those delightful glens, which cut the high table land of the confines of Devon and Cornwall, and opening each through its gorge of down and rock, towards the boundless Western Ocean,

Each is like the other, and each is like no other English scenery. Each
has its upright walls inland of rich oak wood, nearer the sea of dark
green furze, then of smooth turf, then of weird black cliffs which
range out right and left far into the deep sea, in castles, spires, and
wings of jagged iron stone. Each has its narrow strip of fertile meadow,
its crystal trout stream winding across and across from one hill foot to
the other; its grey stone mill, with the water sparkling and humming
round the dripping wheels: its dark rock pool above the tide mark,
where the salmon trout gather in from their Atlantic wanderings, after
each autumn flood: its ridge of blown sand, bright with golden trefoil
and crimson lady's fingers; its grey bank of polished pebbles down
which the stream rattles toward the sea below. Each has its black field
of jagged shark's teeth rock which paves the cove from side to side . . .
stretching in parallel lines out to the westward, in strata set upright on
edge, or tilted toward each other at strange angles by primeval earthquakes;—such is the 'Mouth'—as those coves are called; and such the
jaw of teeth which they display, one rasp of which would grind abroad
the timbers of the stoutest ship. To landward, all richness, softness,
and peace; to seaward, a waste and howling wilderness of rock and
roller, barren to the fisherman, and hopeless to the shipwrecked
mariner.

In only one of these 'Mouths' is a landing for boats made possible by
a long sea wall of rock, which protects it from the rollers of the
Atlantic, and that mouth is Marsland.

Eustace did not find himself alone at Marsland, for on that
October night of the full moon Rose Salterne had chosen to
walk naked in the sea, counselled by the white witch Lucy Passmore, who assured her that only thus would she see the face of
her future husband in her mirror. The scene of Rose's midnight
bathe was one that Kingsley enjoyed painting:

Rose went faltering down the strip of sand, some twenty yards farther,
and there, slipping off her clothes, stood shivering and trembling for a
moment before she entered the sea. She was between two walls of
rock: that on her left hand some twenty feet high hid her in deepest
shade; that on her right, though much lower, took the whole blaze of
the midnight moon. Great festoons of live and purple sea-weed hung
from it, shading dark cracks and crevices, fit haunts for all the goblins
of the sea. On her left hand, the peaks of the rock frowned down

ghastly black; on her right hand, far aloft, the downs slept bright and cold.

The breeze had died away; not even a roller broke the perfect stillness of the cove. The gulls were all asleep upon the ledges. Over all was a true autumn silence; a silence which may be heard. She stood awed, and listened in hope of a sound which might tell her that any living thing beside herself existed.

There was a faint bleat, as of a new born lamb, high above her head; she started and looked up. Then a wail from the cliffs, as of a child in pain, answered by another from the opposite rocks. They were but the passing snipe and the otter calling to her brood; but to her they were mysterious, supernatural goblins, come to answer to her call. Nevertheless, they only quickened her expectations; and the witch had told her not to fear them. If she performed the rite duly, nothing would harm her: but she could hear the beating of her own heart, as she stepped, mirror in hand, into the cold water, waded hastily, as far as she dare, and then stopped aghast.

A ring of flame was round her waist; every limb was bathed in lambent light; all the multitudinous life of the autumn sea, stirred by her approach had flashed suddenly into glory . . . She could see every shell which crawled on the white sand at her feet, every rock fish which played in and out of the crannies, and stared at her with its broad bright eyes; while the great palmate oarweeds which waved along the chasm, half seen in the glimmering water, seemed to beckon her down with long brown hands to a grave amid their chilly bowers. She turned to flee; but she had gone too far now to retreat; hastily dipping her head three times, she hurried out to the sea marge and looking, through her dripping locks at the magic mirror, pronounced the incantation—

> A maiden pure, here I stand,
> Neither on sea, nor yet on land;
> Angels watch me on either hand.
> If you be landsman, come down the strand;
> If you be sailor, come up the sand;
> If you be angel, come from the sky,
> Look in my glass, and pass me by;
> Look in my glass, and go from the shore;
> Leave me, but love me for evermore.

The incantation was hardly finished; her eyes were straining into the mirror, where as may be supposed, nothing appeared but the sparkle of the drips from her own tresses, when she heard rattling down the pebbles the hasty feet of men and horses.

The riders who had so rudely disturbed Rose's spell were none other than the two Jesuits on their way to Ireland, and the wounded Eustace. It was a night of ill omen for the poor girl, for it was events in Ireland that were to bring about her ruin.

For the time, however, Rose Salterne's star seemed to be in the ascendant. Before leaving to fight in the Irish wars, eight of her admirers, all young men from the best Devon families, formed themselves into the Brotherhood of the Rose at a tavern on Bideford Quay. There, while feasting on 'Clovelly herrings and Torridge salmon, Exmoor mutton and Stow venison' Amyas and Frank Leigh, Will Cary, and the heirs of the Basset, Fortescue, Chichester, St Leger and Coffin families plighted their troths to the mayor's lovely daughter. Next day they left for Ireland, and it was from there that Amyas brought back as prisoner the Spanish nobleman who was to prove the downfall of himself and Rose.

Don Guzman Maria Magdalena Soto mayor de Soto was a true *hidalgo*. 'He was an exceedingly tall and graceful personage, of that *sangre azul* which marked high Visi-gothic descent; golden haired and fair skinned, with hands as small and white as a woman's; his lips were delicate, but thin, and compressed closely at the corner of the mouth; and his pale blue eye had a glassy dullness. In spite of his beauty and his carriage, Amyas shrank from him instinctively.'

Don Guzman was taken to live as a prisoner with Sir Richard Grenville while his ransom money was collected. The famous Grenville house at Stowe had been a ruin even in Kingsley's day, but he conveyed a picture of it from old records:

The old house . . . was a huge rambling building, half castle, half dwelling house, such as may be seen still (almost a unique specimen) in Compton Castle near Torquay, the dwelling of Humphrey Gilbert . . .

On three sides, to the north, west, and south, the lofty walls of the old ballium still stood, with their machicolated turrets, loopholes, and dark downward crannies for dropping stones and fire on the besiegers, the relics of a more unsettled age: but the southern court of the ballium had become a flower garden, with quaint terraces, statues, knots of flowers, clipped yews and hollies, and all the pedantries of the topiarian art. And toward the east, where the vista of the valley opened, the old walls were gone, and the frowning Norman keep, ruined in the Wars of the Roses, had been replaced by the rich and stately architecture of the Tudors. . . .

From the house, on three sides, the hill sloped steeply down, and the garden, where Sir Richard and Amyas were walking, gave a truly English prospect. At one time they could catch, over the western walls, a glimpse of the blue ocean flecked with passing sails; and at the next, spread far below them, range on range of fertile park, stately avenue, yellow autumn woodland, and purple heather moors, lapping over and over each other up the valley to the old British earthwork, which stood black and furze grown on its conical peak and, standing out against the sky on the highest bank of hill which closed the valley to the east, the lofty tower of Kilkhampton church, rich with the monuments and offerings of five centuries of Grenvils.

Had Don Guzman remained within the pleasant confines of Stowe, all might have been well. But he was invited to dinner by the Mayor of Bideford. Mr Salterne lived in Bridgeland Street, which was not then the splendid thoroughfare that it later became. In those days it was chiefly flanked by rope walks and sailmakers' shops. But there were one or two fine houses in it and the mayor kept sufficient state to satisfy the Spaniard who derived more pleasure, however, from the beauty of the lovely Rose, and immediately fell in love with her. For many months the affair went unnoticed, for the eight members of the Brotherhood of the Rose were sailing the seven seas at the time, but in the summer of 1583 Will Cary, now a lieutenant in her majesty's Irish army, came home on leave and was invited to dinner at Annery House, on the banks of the Torridge, upstream from Bideford Bridge.

Annery played a brief but important part in the story of *Westward Ho!* Kingsley probably dragged it in because he was anxious to write about his wife's family, the St Legers. The Mr St Leger who lived at Annery in Elizabethan times was a brother of Sir Richard Grenville's wife. He had recently been entertained to dinner by the trustees of Bideford Bridge, and 'between him and one of the bridge trustees arose an argument, whether a salmon caught below the bridge was better or worse than one caught above; and as that weighty question could only be decided by practical experience, Mr St Leger vowed that as the bridge had given him a good dinner, he would give the bridge one, and offered a bet of five pounds that he would find them, out of the pool below Annery, as firm and flaky a salmon as the Appledore one which they had just eaten; and then, in the fulness of his heart, invited the whole company present to dine with him at Annery three days after, and bring with them each a wife or daughter; and Don Guzman being at table, he was invited too.

'So there was a mighty feast in the great hall at Annery, such as had seldom been seen since Judge Hankford feasted Edward the Fourth there; and while everyone was eating their best and drinking their worst, Rose Salterne and Don Guzman were pretending not to see each other, and watching each other all the more.'

After the feast the ladies strolled in the gardens by the river. 'It was a beautiful sight, the great terrace at Annery that afternoon; with the smart dames in their gaudy dresses parading up and down in twos and three before the stately house; or looking down upon the park, with the old oaks and the deer, and the broad land-locked river spread out like a lake beneath, all bright in the glare of the midsummer sun.'

One lady, however, was missing from the company, and that was Rose Salterne. Her absence was observed by Lady Grenville, who went in search of her, accompanied by Will Cary. 'So they

went down past the herds of deer, by a path into the lonely dell
where stood the fatal oak . . .' Suddenly, 'Cary grasped Lady
Grenvil's hand so tightly that she gave a little shriek of pain.
' "There they are!" whispered he, heedless of her; and pointed
to the oak where, half hidden by the tall fern, stood Rose and the
Spaniard. Her head was on his bosom.'

There was no alternative but to fight a duel the following day.
Both gentlemen in fact survived the combat with their honour
and their skins intact, but Don Guzman could no longer remain
in the country. His ransom money was paid and he stole away
secretly one night with Rose and her accomplice, Lucy Passmore,
the white witch of Marsland. After a night in a cottage built into
the ruins of Marisco Castle on Lundy Island, they sailed for
Caracas where the don was to take up a governorship.

Most of the second half of *Westward Ho!* concerned the
attempts of Amyas Leigh and his companions to rescue Rose
from her South American prison. After two hundred pages of
these adventures, Kingsley describes the ship's return:

It is the evening of the 15th of February 1587, and Mrs Leigh . . . is
pacing slowly up and down the terrace walk at Burrough, looking out
over the winding river, and the hazy sand hills, and the wide western
sea, as she has done every evening, be it fair weather or foul, for three
weary years. . . . But this evening Northam is in a stir. The pebble
ridge is thundering far below as it thundered years ago; but Northam
is noisy enough without the rolling of the surge. The tower is rocking
with the pealing bells: the people are all in the streets shouting and
singing round bonfires. They are burning the pope in effigy . . . The
hills are red with bonfires in every village; and far away the bells of
Bideford are answering the bells of Northam, as they answered them
seven years ago, when Amyas returned from sailing round the world.
For this day has come the news that Mary Queen of Scots is beheaded
in Fotheringay; and all England, like a dreamer who shakes off some
hideous nightmare, has leapt up in one tremendous shout of jubilation,
as the error and the danger of seventeen anxious years is lifted from its
heart for ever.

But still the bells pealed on and would not cease.

(*above left*) 28 Mill Street, Bideford, the home of Edward Capern, the poet-postman

(*above right*) Statue of Charles Kingsley at Bideford

(*left*) Kingsley Cottage, Clovelly

Aerial view of Lundy

What was that which answered them from afar out of the fast darkening twilight? A flash, and then the thunder of a gun at sea.

Mrs Leigh stopped. The flash was right outside the Bar. A ship in distress it could not be. The wind was light and westerly. It was a high spring tide, as evening floods are always there. What could it be? Another flash, another gun. The noisy folks of Northam were hushed at once, and all hurried into the churchyard which looks down on the broad flats and the river.

There was a gallant ship outside the Bar. She was running in, too, with all sails set. A large ship; nearly a thousand tons she might be . . .

Round the Hubbastone she came at last. There was music on board, drums and fifes, shawms and trumpets, which wakened ringing echoes from every knoll of wood and slab of slate. And as she opened full on Burrough House, another cheer burst from her crew, and rolled up to the hills from off the silver waters far below, full a mile away. Mrs Leigh walked quickly toward the house, and called her maid. 'Grace, bring me my hood. Master Amyas is come home.'

Amyas had sad news for his mother. Both Frank and Rose Salterne had been burnt at the stake by the Spanish Inquisition. In their place he had brought a beautiful savage called Ayacanora* whom he had rescued from the jungle banks of the river Meta. She 'was an Indian girl; and yet, when he looked again,—was it an Indian girl? Amyas had seen hundreds of those delicate dark skinned daughters of the forest, but never such a one as this. Her stature was taller, her limbs were fuller and more rounded; her complexion, though tanned by light, was fairer by far than his own sunburnt face; her hair, crowned with a garland of white flowers, was not lank, and straight, and black, like an Indian's, but of a rich glossy brown, and curling richly and crisply from her very temples to her knees.'

Ayacanora was in fact none other than the daughter of the swaggering Captain Oxenham whose gunner, Salvation Yeo, had given Amyas the carved buffalo horn. She was the child of his Spanish mistress, but had been brought up by Indians and was

---

* The inspiration for the character of Ayacanora probably came from 'Ralegh', the first Indian to be baptised in an English church, who must have been brought to England at about the same time as the fictional Ayacanora.

as savage as they. Amyas handed her over to his mother to tame, and the three of them settled down at Burrough, but only for a time.

The final pages of the book depict the defeat and pursuit of the great Armada. Amyas was in command of one of the ships from Bideford that joined the famous battle in the Channel. After the many days of desperate fighting had ended in an English victory, he singled out Don Guzman's ship, the *Santa Catharina*, to pursue westward round Land's End. When the hunt was at its height a blinding storm broke.

She swung round. The masts bent like whips; crack went the foresail like a cannon. What matter. Within two hundred yards of them was the Spaniard; in front of her, and above her, a huge dark bank rose through the dense hail . . .

'What is it? Morte? Hartland?'

'It might be anything for thirty miles.'

'Lundy!' said Yeo. 'The south end! I see the head of the Shutter in the breakers! Hard a-port yet, and get her close-hauled as you can and the Lord have mercy on us still! Look at the Spaniard!'

'Yes, look at the Spaniard!'

On their left hand, as they broached-to, the wall of granite sloped down from the clouds toward an isolated peak of rock, some two hundred feet in height. Then a hundred yards of roaring breaker upon a sunken shelf, across which the face of the tide poured like a cataract; then, amid a column of salt smoke, the Shutter, like a huge black fang, rose waiting for its prey; and between the Shutter and the land, the great galleon loomed dimly through the storm.

He, too, had seen his danger, and tried to broach-to. But her clumsy mass refused to obey the helm; he struggled a moment, half hid in foam; fell away again, and rushed upon his doom.

'Lost! lost!' cried Amyas madly, and throwing up his hands, let go the tiller. Yeo caught it just in time.

'Sir! sir! What are you at? We shall clear the rock yet.'

'Yes!' shouted Amyas in his frenzy; 'but he will not!'

Another minute. The galleon gave a sudden jar, and stopped. Then one long heave and bound, as if to free herself. And then her bows lighted clear upon the Shutter.

An awful silence fell on every English soul. They heard not the roaring of wind and surge; they saw not the blinding flashes of the lightning; but they heard one long ear piercing wail to every saint in heaven rise from five hundred human throats; they saw the mighty ship heel over from the wind, and sweep headlong down the cataract of the race, plunging her yards into the foam, and showing her whole black side even to her keel, till she rolled clean over, and vanished for ever and ever.

'Shame!' cried Amyas, hurling his sword far into the sea, 'to lose my right, my right! When it was in my very grasp! Unmerciful!'

A crack which rent the sky, and made the granite ring and quiver; a bright world of flame, and then a blank of utter darkness, against which stood out, glowing red hot, every mast, and sail, and rock, and Salvation Yeo, as he stood just in front of Amyas, the tiller in his hand. All red-hot transfigured into fire; and behind, the black, black night.

Amyas's victory was a hollow one. The flash of lightning that illuminated Don Guzman's sinking ship deprived him of his sight and left him a broken man. In the last great scene of the book he asked Will Cary to lead him to a point overhanging the western cliffs of Lundy and there, staring down into the sea with sightless eyes, he was reconciled with the enemy who lay beneath it.

It was no easy matter to find a safe place; for from the foot of the crag the heathery turf slopes down . . . on one side to a cliff which overhangs a shoreless cove of deep dark sea, and on the other to an abyss even more hideous, where the solid rock has sunk away, and opened inland in the hillside a smooth walled pit, some sixty feet square and some hundred and fifty in depth, aptly known then as now, as the Devil's limekiln, the mouth of which, as old wives say, was once closed by the Shutter rock itself, till the fiend in malice hurled it into the sea, to be a pest to mariners. A narrow and untrodden cavern at the bottom connects it with the outer sea; they could even then hear the mysterious thunder and gurgle of the surge in the subterranean adit, as it rolled huge boulders to and fro in darkness, and forced before it gusts of pent up air. It was a spot to curdle weak blood, and to make weak heads reel: but all the fitter on that account for Amyas and his fancy . . .

Cary and Jack looked at him, and then at each other. His eyes were clear, and bright, and full of meaning; and yet they knew that he was blind. His voice was shaping itself into song. Was he inspired? Insane? What was it? And they listened with awe struck faces, as the giant pointed down into the blue depths far below, and went on.

'And I saw him sitting in his cabin, like a valiant gentleman of Spain, and his officers were sitting round him, with their swords upon the table at the wine. And the prawns and the crayfish . . . swam in and out above their heads: but Don Guzman he never heeded, but sat still, and drank his wine. Then he took a locket from his bosom; and I heard him speak, Will, and he said: "Here's the picture of my fair and true lady; drink to her, Señors all." Then he spoke to me, Will, and called me, right up through the oarweed and the sea: "We have had a fair quarrel, Señor; it is time to be friends once more. My wife and your brother have forgiven me; so your honour takes not stain." And I answered, We are friends, Don Guzman. God has judged our quarrel, and not we. Then he said, "I have sinned, and I am punished." And I said, And, Señor, so am I. Then he held out his hand to me, Cary, and I stooped to take it, and awoke.'

Ever since *Westward Ho!* was published, it has been a favourite game of pedants to pick holes in its historical accuracy. The champions of Barnstaple have never ceased to complain of the starring role given to Bideford in the book, and Kingsley was certainly unfortunate to become involved in the rivalry between the two towns which is so intense that map makers, for fear of offending either party, name the great bay on which they stand 'Barnstaple or Bideford Bay' to this day. Ten years after the publication of *Westward Ho!* Kingsley was still answering indignant letters from Barnstaple men. His best-informed critic was a West Country historian called Cotton who insisted, in a lecture, that it was Barnstaple, not Bideford, that manned and fitted out the ships that helped defeat the Armada. Kingsley surrendered the point unconditionally. 'I wrote *Westward Ho!* without any access to town records, much more to state papers, chiefly by the light of my dear old Hakluyt. I had always been puzzled by the small mention of Barnstaple in the documents which I knew.'*

But attacks have continued to be launched ever since. Bideford, as R. P. Chope† pointed out in 1912, was only a third of the size of Barnstaple in the 1570s, with a population of 1,500, and was not to become a port of any note until the trade in Virginia tobacco and Newfoundland cod developed a hundred years later. Arthur H. Norway‡ echoed Chope's opinion, though, in Kingsley's defence, he added, 'I could never find anything in Barnstaple that repaid the trouble of going there.'

In recent years W. G. Hoskins, a brilliant historian with access to newly discovered records, has done much to put the record straight on Kingsley's behalf. In 1573 Bideford was, it seems, a more important place than had been supposed. In that year it was judged worthy to emerge from under the wing of the Grenville family and be granted a charter of incorporation from the queen. This recognised its inhabitants as citizens of a 'free burgh' with the right to receive 'all the issues of their town to their own use . . . to have mayor bailiff and other offices, to be chosen of their own body . . . to have a mace, fine gowns and other gayeties'.§ The cause of Bideford's increased importance at this time was Sir Richard Grenville's colonisation of Virginia and Carolina, and the establishment of a brisk tobacco trade many years earlier than had been supposed. By 1570 a fleet of fifty ships was also sailing to the Newfoundland Banks every year. Fifty years earlier Leland had already remarked on Bideford's shipbuilding activities, praising 'a praty quic Streate of Smithes and other Occupiers for Ship crafte beyond the bridge'.

Yet Hoskins would be the last to deny that the peak of Bideford prosperity was not reached until the 1680s, when her mono-

---

* Much light on the Elizabethan period was to be shed shortly when Kingsley's brother-in-law, J. A. Froude, published his *History of England.*

† R. P. Chope, 'The Historical Basis of Kingsley's *Westward Ho!*' in *Devonian Year Book* (London Devonian Association, 1912).

‡ Arthur H. Norway, *Highways and Byways in Devon and Cornwall.*

§ Thomas Madox, *Firma Burgi* (1726).

poly of the tobacco trade reached its height, and she far surpassed Barnstaple as the largest port in North Devon. It was in this period, too, that two of her most famous features, the riverside quay and Bridgeland Street were built.

One can pick out small historical inaccuracies from *Westward Ho!* for as long as it amuses one: the Leighs lived at Tonacombe, for instance, and not at Burrough:* the Cary who was at Clovelly Court in the late sixteenth century was a Richard and not a William, and he was a lawyer and not a seaman; there was no grammar school at Bideford before 1657.† But *Westward Ho!* was, after all, a historical novel and not a history book. If it is insecure historically, it is remarkably sound topographically. The Rev R. S. Hawker of Morwenstow, it is true, remarked to a friend, 'You would have grievously failed in your search for the localities referred to, but by no means identified, in *Westward Ho!*' but as usual he did Kingsley less than justice. The novel gives a picture of North Devon that is not only extraordinarily beautiful, but also accurate.

* Burrough was the home of the famous merchant-adventurer, Stephen Burrough.
† R. P. Chope, 'The Historical Basis of Kingsley's *Westward Ho!*' in *Devonian Year Book* (London Devonian Association, 1912).

Chapter 6

'Two Years Ago'

Two years after he left Bideford in 1855, Kingsley wrote a novel about Clovelly called *Two Years Ago*. He gave it this title because it dealt with the period of the Crimean War, to which its hero, Tom Thurnall, vanished towards the end of the book. Tom Thurnall was a much travelled doctor with a special interest in cholera, a character probably based on Kingsley's brother George, with a slight admixture of Dr Ackland of Bideford. He arrived at Clovelly (renamed Aberalva) by means of one of the west coast shipwrecks that had haunted Kingsley's imagination ever since his boyhood. This particular wreck was on the infamous Clovelly rocks known as the Chough and Crow, and was observed from the Deer Park cliffs by a poet called Elsley Vavasour, the fictional tenant of Clovelly Court (renamed Penalva Court).

Tom Thurnall, the sole survivor, managed to struggle ashore with his wordly fortune, a bag of Australian gold, still strapped to his belt. When he saw, the next day, the enchanted shore on which fate had thrown him, he decided to stay in Aberalva. After reading Kingsley's description of the place, no reader would blame him:

> In going up Aberalva Street, you remark several things; first, that the houses were all whitewashed yesterday, except where the snowy white is picked out by buttresses of pink and blue; next, that they all have bright green palings in front, and bright green window sills and frames; next, that they are all roofed with shining gray slate, and the

space between the window and the pales flagged with the same; next, that where such space is not flagged, it is full of flowers and shrubs which stand the winter only in our greenhouses. The fuchsias are ten feet high, laden with ripe purple berries (for there are no birds to pick them off); and there, in the front of the coast-guard lieutenant's house is *Cobaea scandens*, covered with purple claret glasses, as it has been ever since Christmas, for Aberalva knows no winter; and there are grown up men in it who never put on a skate, or made a snowball in their lives. A most cleanly, bright-coloured, foreign-looking street, is that long straggling one which runs up the hill towards Penalva Court: only remark, that this cleanliness is gained by making the gutter in the middle street the common sewer of the town, and tread clear of cabbage leaves, pilchard bones *et id genus omne*. For Aberalva is like Paris (if the answer of a celebrated sanitary reformer to the Emperor be truly reported), 'fair without but foul within'.

It was not only the houses of Aberalva that charmed Thurnall, but their inhabitants, the fishermen. Kingsley took his hero (and his readers) down to the harbour to meet these Sea Titans in their red caps, blue jackets, striped jerseys and bright brown trousers:

Let us go on, and up the street, after we have scrambled through the usual labyrinth of timber-baulks, rusty anchors, boats which have been dragged, for the purposes of mending and tarring, into the very middle of the road, and old spars stowed under walls, in the vain hope that they may be of some use for something some day, and withstand the stares and welcomes of the lazy giants who are sitting about upon them, black locked, black bearded, with ruddy, wholesome faces, and eyes as bright as diamonds; men who are on their own ground, and know it; who will not touch their caps to you, or pull the short black pipe from between their lips as you pass, but expect you to prove yourself a gentleman, by speaking respectfully to them; which, if you do, you will find them as hearty, intelligent, brave fellows as ever walked this earth, capable of anything, from working the naval brigade guns of Sevastopol down to running up to a hundred miles in a cockleshell lugger, to forestall the early mackerel market.

Tom Thurnall set up a practice in the village, and, in the course of visiting his patients in outlying farms, learned to love the surrounding countryside. One such visit was described in detail. Those with knowledge of the area will recognise Welsford Moor:

> Thurnall started, one bright Sunday evening, to see a sick child at an upland farm, some few miles from the town. And partly because he liked the walk, and partly because he could no other, having neither horse nor gig, he went on foot; and whistled as he went, like any throstle cock, along the pleasant vale, by flowery banks and ferny wall, by oak and ash and thorn, while Alva flashed and swirled between green boughs below, clear coffee brown from last night's rain. Some miles up the turnpike road he went, and then away to the right, through the ash woods of Trebooze, up by the rill which drips from pool to pool over the ledges of grey slate, deep embedded in dark sedge, and broad bright burdock leaves, and tall angelica and tufts of king, and crown and lady-fern, and all the demi-tropic luxuriance of the fat western soil, and steaming western woods; out onto the boggy moor at the glen head ... where the turf is enamelled with the hectic marsh violet, and the pink pimpernel, and the blue bells and green heads of the ivy-leaved campanula; out upon the steep smooth down above, and away over the broad cattle pastures; and then to pause a moment, and look far and wide over land and sea.
>
> It was a 'day of God'. The earth lay like one great emerald, ringed and roofed with sapphire; blue sea, blue mountain, blue sky overhead. There she lay, not sleeping, but basking in her quiet Sabbath joy.

Yet all was not well in this earthly paradise. Behind the whitewashed walls of the fishermen's cottages at Aberalva was filth and decay upon which the germs of cholera were breeding. Thurnall feared the possibility of an outbreak in the hot summer of 1854, and set to work to clean up the cottages. Kingsley himself had seen Dr Ackland's equally fruitless attempts to implement the Removal of Public Nuisances Act in Bridgeland Street in July 1854.

Thurnall discovered, when it came to converting the landlords to his way of thinking, that it was greed and laziness that chiefly prevented them from cleaning up the cottages they owned. In 'the Great Trebooze of Trebooze', Kingsley portrayed a man who was presumably a typical Devonshire squire of the period: 'A small squireen, cursed with six or seven hundred a year of his own, never sent to school, college, or into the army, he had grown up in a narrow circle of squireens like himself, without an object save that of gratifying his animal passions; and had, about six years before, being then just of age, settled in life by marrying his housemaid—the only wise thing, perhaps he ever did. For she, a clever and determined woman, kept him, though not from drunkenness and debt, at least from *delirium tremens* and ruin . . .'

Tom went to see Trebooze, but he received a brief answer to his inquiries about sanitation:

'Mr. Trebooze, you are a man of position in the county, and own some houses in Aberalva. Don't you think you could use your influence in this matter?'

'Own some houses! yes!' and Mr. Trebooze consigned the said cottages to a variety of unmentionable places; 'cost me more in rates than they bring in in rent, even if I get the rent paid. I should like to get a six-pounder and blow the whole lot into the sea.'

Needless to say Kingsley's own heart was as much in this matter of sanitary reform as was that of Tom Thurnall. Indeed he put words into Thurnall's mouth that summed up his own obsession with cleanliness: 'I hate to see a speck of dirt in the street; I hate to see a woman's gown torn; I hate to see her stockings down at heel; I hate to see anything wasted, anything awry, anything wrong; I hate to see water-power wasted, manure wasted, land wasted, muscle wasted, pluck wasted, brains wasted.'

All Tom Thurnall's warnings were ignored. In the cottages the drains were left blocked and, worse still, in the fish jowder's court, the piles of cod's entrails rotted. And so, as the doctor had foretold, in the blazing days of July, Baalzebub commenced his banquet of human flesh.

He had come at last, Baalzebub, god of flies, and god of filth; he had come to visit his self-blinded worshippers, and bestow on them his own Cross of the Legion of Dishonour. He had come suddenly, capriciously, sportively, as he sometimes comes; as he had come to Newcastle the summer before, while yet the rest of England was untouched. He had wandered all but harmless about the West Country that summer; as if his maw had been full glutted five years before, when he sat for many a week upon the Dartmoor hills, amid the dull brown haze, and sunburnt bents, and dried up water courses of white dusty granite, looking far and wide over the plague struck land, and listening to the dead bell booming all day long in Tavistock churchyard. But he was come at last, with appetite more fierce than ever, and had darted aside to seize on Aberalva, and not to let it go till he had sucked his fill.

All men moved about the streets slowly, fearfully; conscious of some awful presence, which might spring on them from round every corner; some dreadful inevitable spell, which lay upon them like a nightmare weight; and walked to and fro warily, looking anxiously into each other's faces, not to ask 'How are you?' but 'How am I? Do I look as if . . .?'

In the second half of *Two Years Ago* the subject of cholera was abandoned and the castigation of Elsley Vavasour, the poet of Pentalva Court, became the central theme. Kingsley could never resist the temptation to use a novel with a contemporary setting as a platform from which to air his prejudices about the state of the nation. *Yeast* and *Alton Locke* had been virtually pamphlets fulminating against working-class living conditions. In *Two Years Ago* the whipping boys were dirty drains and immoral poets. Elsley was a weak, selfish creature who neglected his wife. The subject of his poetry was not, as it should have been, 'needlewomen and ragged schools, dwellers in Jacob's Island and sleepers under the dry arches of Waterloo Bridge' but the sorrows of distant Italy.* As he grew older his poems lost all purpose, manner took the place of matter and the poetry

* Tennyson always suspected that the character of Vavasour was based on his own, but it is more probable that Shelley was the model.

became 'mere sensuous beauty, mere word-painting'. His own character also degenerated, and he took to opium.

In the last magnificent scenes of the book Kingsley described the poet running amok amid the peaks of the Glyders in North Wales. It may seem strange that the action should be transferred so suddenly away from the West Country. Hartland Point, one feels, in a north-westerly gale, would have made just as impressive a setting for the poet's insanity. The reason for the change of location was, almost certainly, that in the middle of writing the book Kingsley had a holiday in Wales. It was the holiday anticipated in the famous jingle he wrote to his old friend and colleague Tom Hughes:

> Come away with me, Tom,
> Term and talk are done;
> My poor lads are reaping,
> Busy every one.
> Curates mind the parish,
> Sweepers mind the court;
> We'll away to Snowdon
> For our ten days' sport;
> Fish the August evening
> Till the eve is past,
> Whoop like boys, at pounders
> Fairly played and grassed.
> When they cease to dimple.
> Lunge, and swerve, and leap
> Then up over Siabod,
> Choose our nest and sleep.
>
> Down and bathe at day dawn,
> Tramp from lake to lake,
> Washing brain and heart clean
> Every step we take.
> Leave to Robert Browning
> Beggars, fleas, and vines;
> Leave to mournful Ruskin
> Popish Apennines,

'TWO YEARS AGO'

Dirty Stones of Venice
And his Gas-lamps Seven—
We've the stones of Snowdon
And the lamps of heaven.

Once year, like a schoolboys,
Robin-Hooding go,
Leaving fops and fogies
A thousand feet below.

Chapter 7

'The Water-Babies'

Two Years Ago was quickly followed by *The Heroes*, a retelling of the adventures of Perseus, Jason and Theseus, 'men who killed fierce beasts and evil men'. Although the book was naturally set in Ancient Greece, there was more than a splash of the North Devon coast in the tale of Perseus and Andromeda, and, for that matter, in the story of the Argonauts.

The Andromeda myth was one after Kingsley's own heart; a maiden exposed naked all night to the sea spray, awaiting rescue from the jaws of a sea-monster. A few years earlier he had attempted to express what he felt about 'that unfathomable myth' in a figure drawing of the naked Andromeda, but was obliged 'to burn fifty attempts'. Instead he wrote a long poem in Homeric hexameters containing such couplets as:

> They, on the sea girt rock, which is washed by the surge forever
> Set her in silence, the guiltless, aloft with her face to the Eastward

The poem was full of the rhythm of the sea that Kingsley had learned to know so well at Clovelly. It contains a fine description of mermaids:

> Rose from their seaweed chamber the choir of the mystical sea-maids.
> Onward toward her they came, and her heart beat loud at their
>   coming,
> Watching the bliss of the gods, as they wakened the cliffs with their
>   laughter.
> Onward they came in their joy, and before them the roll of the surges...

Coral and sea-fan and tangle, the blooms and the palms of the ocean.
Onward they came in their joy, more white than the foam which
      they scattered,
Laughing and singing, and tossing and twining, while eager, the
      Tritons
Blinded with kisses their eyes, unreproved, and above them in worship
Hovered the terns, and the seagulls swept past them on silvery
      pinions
Echoing softly their laughter; around them the wantoning dolphins
Sighed as they plunged, full of love; and the great sea-horses which
      bore them
Curved up their crests in their pride to the delicate arms of the
      maidens,
Pawing the spray into gems, till a fiery rainfall, unharming,
Sparkled and gleamed on the limbs of the nymphs, and the coils of
      the mermen.

Such erotic delicacies were omitted from the children's version
of the story, which nevertheless retained the flavour of the sea
winds and the salt sea:

And Perseus feared to go inland, but flew along the shore above the
sea; and he went on all the day, and the sky was black with smoke; and
he went on all the night, and the sky was red with flame.

And at the dawn of day he looked toward the cliffs; and at the
water's edge, under a black rock, he saw a white image stand.

'This,' thought he, 'must surely be the statue of some sea-god; I
will go near and see what kind of gods these barbarians worship.'

So he came near; but when he came, it was no statue but a maiden
of flesh and blood; for he could see her tresses streaming in the breeze;
and as he came closer still, he could see how she shrank and shivered
when the waves sprinkled her with cold salt spray . . .

Full of pity and indignation, Perseus drew near and looked upon
the maid. Her cheeks were darker than his were, and her hair was
blue-black like a hyacinth; but Perseus thought 'I have never seen so
beautiful a maiden, not in all our isles. Surely she is a king's daughter.
Do barbarians treat their king's daughters thus? She is too fair, at
least, to have done any wrong. I will speak to her.'

And, lifting the hat from his head, he flashed into her sight. She
shrieked with terror, and tried to hide her face with her hair, for she

could not with her hands; but Perseus cried—

'Do not fear me, fair one; I am a Hellene, and no barbarian. What cruel men have bound you?'

And she answered, weeping—

'I am the daughter of Cepheus, King of Iopa, and my mother is Cassiopoeia of the beautiful tresses, and they called me Andromeda, as long as life was mine. And I stand bound here, hapless that I am, for the sea-monster's food, to atone for my mother's sin. For she boasted of me once that I was fairer than Atergatis, Queen of the Fishes; so she in her wrath sent the sea-floods, and her brother the Fire King sent the earthquakes, and wasted all the land, and after the floods came a monster bred of the slime, who devours all living things. And now he must devour, guiltless though I am—me who never harmed a living thing, nor saw a fish upon the shore but I gave it life, and threw it back into the sea; for in our land we eat no fish, for fear of Atergatis their queen. Yet the priests say that nothing but my blood can atone for a sin which I never committed . . .'

Suddenly looking up she pointed to the sea, and shrieked—

'There he comes, with the sunrise, as they promised. I must die now. How shall I endure it? Oh, go! Is it not dreadful enough to be torn piecemeal without having you to look on?' And she tried to thrust him away . . .

On came the great sea-monster, coasting along like a huge black galley, lazily breasting the ripple, and stopping at times by creek or headland to watch for the laughter of girls at their bleaching, or cattle pawing on the sandhills, or boys bathing on the beach. His great sides were fringed with clustering shells and sea-weeds, and the water gurgled in and out of his wide jaws, as he rolled along, dripping and glistening in the beams of the morning sun.

When *The Heroes* was finished Kingsley wrote nothing for five years. After the spate of books (four in three years)* resulting from his year in Devonshire came a period of drought when, try though he would, he could not get a novel off the ground. It was almost as if, with his departure from the West Country, the sources of his inspiration dried up. When they started to flow again, in 1863, it was, appropriately enough, with *The Water-Babies*.

* *Westward Ho!*; *Glaucus*; *Two Years Ago*; *The Heroes*.

(*above*) Figurehead of the *Caledonian* in Morwenstow churchyard

(*below*) Clovelly Court, Tudor wing

(*above*) Coombe Mill at Coombe Valley

(*below left*) Rose of Torridge Café, formerly the Ship Tavern, Bideford

(*below right*) Bideford Quay and the bridge

This was to be Kingsley's last work of fiction, with the exception of *Hereward the Wake* published in 1867. It was intended for his youngest son Grenville. The story of how *The Water-Babies* came to be written is well known. One fine spring in 1862 Fanny reminded Charles of an old promise: 'Rose, Maurice and Mary have got their book,' she said, 'and baby must have his.' Kingsley made no answer but, barely stopping to finish his breakfast, he locked himself in his study and returned half an hour later with the first chapter of *The Water-Babies*.

The book was an instant success and has become one of that select group of Victorian children's books on sale in every chain store. It has gone into close on a hundred editions and is still available in nine of them. And its subject again was the sea. But this time Kingsley described not the surface of the sea, but life underneath it. As we read it we are reminded of those longings he had so often expressed when in the West Country to dive down under the surface of the water and lose himself there. In *Westward Ho!* he had tentatively explored the possibilities of the subaquatic world, when he described Don Guzman at wine in the cabin of his sunken ship. In *Glaucus* he related the fable of the old Greek fisherman after whom the book was named, who after 'eating of the herb which gave his fish strength to leap back into their native element, he was seized on the spot with a strange longing to follow them under the waves, and become for ever a companion of the fair semi-human forms with which the Hellenic poets peopled their sunny bays and firths, feeding "silent flocks" far below on the green Zostera beds, or basking with them on the sunny ledges in the summer noon, or wandering in the still bays on sultry nights amid the choir of Amphitrite and her sea-nymphs.'

In *The Water-Babies* Kingsley finally took the plunge, for, apart from the first chapter, most of the story takes place under the water. The hero of *The Water-Babies* is, of course, Tom, the 'climbing boy', whose real life story was always said to have been based on that of James Seward, the boy who swept the chimneys at Eversley, and eventually became an alderman of the neighbouring town of Wokingham. In an interview given to a newspaper after Kingsley was dead, Seward described his sufferings:

> What do you think of having straw lighted under you and pins stuck into your feet to force you up a chimney? Yet that is what happened to me, and I have known what it was to come down the dark flue not only covered with soot, but with blood also, from the rough climbing with knees and hands and elbows.
>
> It is impossible to exaggerate the sufferings of the climbing-boys in those days, and they show how hardly industrial freedom has been won, and why men are jealous of any encroachment upon it. Terrible cruelty was inflicted. It was a common practice to steep these little slaves of the brush in strong brine to harden their flesh. In my own case, my master used soda. Nor was it a case of up and down in a few minutes. Sometimes I used to stay up a difficult chimney five or six hours at a stretch. It is a wonder, when I think of it to-day, how I survived it.

To Kingsley, Seward's story summed up all the filth and injustice of the industrial age, and he felt that only water could wash away such sin, and the water he chose was Devonshire water. Admittedly the river into which Tom first fell was a Yorkshire one, for Tom was a Yorkshire lad and he had just escaped his pursuers by climbing down the precipitous side of Malham Cove which is in Yorkshire. Once he started his underwater life, however, the location of the river changed.

Kingsley wrote much of the book on the banks of the Itchen at Alresford, near Winchester, where he was the guest of the wealthy landowner F. J. P. Marx at Arlebury Park, Itchen Abbas.* The waters of the Itchen at this point were so clear that 'none could see where the water ended and where the air began'.† But, as it approached the sea, Tom's river must have changed its name once more, for a monster that he met in it was never

---

* I am indebted to Anthony Brodie for this information.
† Charles Kingsley, *Hereward the Wake*.

seen at Alresford. 'Such a fish! ten times as big as the biggest trout, and a hundred times as big as Tom, sculling up the stream past him, as easily as Tom had sculled down.

'Such a fish! shining silver from head to tail, and here and there a crimson dot; with a grand hooked nose, and grand curling lip, and a grand bright eye . . .'

Tom was now, surely, in the Torridge, and what he had just met was one of the famous Torridge salmon on its way upstream to breed. The first and last verses of a poem Kingsley included in *The Water-Babies* is almost certainly a portrait of the beloved Devonshire river.

> Clear and cool, clear and cool,
> By laughing shallow, and dreaming pool;
> Cool and clear, cool and clear,
> By shining shingle, and foaming weir;
> Under the crag where the ouzel sings,
> And the ivied wall where the church-bell rings,
> Undefiled, for the undefiled;
> Play by me, bathe in me, mother and child.
>
> Dank and foul, dank and foul,
> By the smoky town in its murky cowl;
> Foul and dank, foul and dank,
> By wharf and sewer and slimy bank;
> Darker and darker the farther I go,
> Baser and baser the richer I grow;
> Who dare sport with the sin-defiled?
> Shrink from me, turn from me, mother and child.
>
> Strong and free, strong and free,
> The floodgates are open, away from the sea.
> Free and strong, free and strong,
> Cleansing my streams as I hurry along
> To the golden sands, and the leaping bar,
> And the taintless tide that awaits me afar,
> As I lose myself in the infinite main,
> Like a soul that has sinned and is pardoned again.

Undefiled, for the undefiled;
Play by me, bathe in me, mother and child.

And when Tom finally crossed the 'leaping bar', it was surely the Bideford bar he crossed, and the Bideford bell buoy he sat upon.

The red buoy was in sight, dancing in the open sea; and to the buoy he would go, and to it he went. He passed great shoals of bass and mullet, leaping and rushing in after the shrimps, but he never heeded them or they him; and once he passed a great black shining seal, who was coming in after the mullet. The seal put his head and shoulders out of water, and stared at him, looking exactly like a fat old greasy Negro with a grey pate . . .

The sea-breeze came in freshly with the tide, and blew the fog away; and the little waves danced for joy around the buoy, and the old buoy danced with them. The shadows of the clouds ran races over the bright blue bay, and yet never caught each other up; and the breakers plunged merrily upon the wide white sands, and jumped up over the rocks, to see what the green fields inside were like, and tumbled down and broke themselves all to pieces, and never minded it a bit, but mended themselves and jumped up again. And the terns hovered over Tom like huge white dragonflies with black heads, and the gulls laughed like girls at play, and the sea-pies, with their red bills and legs flew to and fro from shore to shore, and whistled sweet and wild.

Chapter 8

North Devon Today

It is over a hundred years since Charles Kingsley saw Devon. If he were to return now he would, one suspects, be pleased by the changes he saw rather than the reverse. The north coast, by contrast with the south, remains comparatively unspoiled. The great luxury hotels of the gin-and-tonic belt have never gone up, the great main roads have not yet come down* and the railways have actually receded—Bideford station is now closed and the line only runs as far as Barnstaple. The people of Devon, while they have lost nothing of the warmth and poetry for which Kingsley loved them, lead easier and more comfortable lives than they did in his day, and the terrible death toll that the sea took of fishermen and sailors is now greatly reduced, partly as a result of the heroic work of the air-sea rescue service operating from Chivenor.

The countryside remains much the same, 'wide, buzzard-haunted, remote and withdrawn from the . . . lunacies of the modern world'.† The age-old process of enclosure has, admittedly, continued. Kingsley, in *Westward Ho!*, observed that in his day there were more green squares of pasture on the brown of the moorland than in Elizabethan times. Now there are still more. Indeed not far from Clovelly a contemporary of Kingsley commemorated his piece of land reclamation with a pair of ornate gates fit for the approach to a stately home. There has

---

* There is a plan to run a spur road to Barnstaple from the M5 motorway.
† W. G. Hoskins, *Devon*.

also been some afforestation, particularly in the area of Bursdon Moor. These agricultural advances would have pleased Kingsley, for he longed to see the barren moorland become fertile. Much of it, fortunately, remains barren.*

Neither have the men who farm the fertile valleys changed much since Kingsley's day or, for that matter, Queen Elizabeth I's. Milk remains their chief produce. Devon is the leading milk-producing area of the British Isles and vast Unigate tankers collect Devonshire milk daily. This is now extracted from the cows by machine, but in many other matters men on the smaller farms prefer to do things the way 'gramfer' did. And they still speak in the old Devon way, asking you, 'Where are you to?' meaning, 'Where are you from?' A few are still deeply superstitious, like Amyas Leigh, who 'devoutly believed in fairies, whom he called pixies; and held that they changed babies, and made the mushroom rings on the downs to dance in'. One farmer living near the Cornish border is convinced that he has been pixie led, and knows that the cure is to turn his coat. If you mention that his coat is inside out he will give you 'the sideways look'. Another farmer goes regularly to a charmer to have his warts cured.

Tourism has brought about the only major change in this part of the world. As a Christian Socialist, Kingsley would no doubt have derived satisfaction from the thought that factory workers from Cardiff and London can now afford to be 're-magnetised' on the shores of the Atlantic, even if their presence does necessitate occasional fields bearing crops of little else but caravans. A Devonshire friend writes, 'One cannot drive down the roughest country lane without seeing the sign designed to attract the tourist. In its simplest form it is a badly scrawled "B and B" (over which a sack is tied with bailer twine when the house is full). But it progresses through "Bed and Breakfast, Evening

---

* Kingsley was mistaken in supposing that these moors could ever become fertile. The topsoil is thin and lies above feet of undrainable clay.

Meal" to the professionally painted sign "Accommodation, Evening Meal, Central Heating, No Vacancies", with a little door which slides over the "No" if a visitor has suddenly cancelled.'*

Food at these farmhouses is plentiful and cheap. Visitors may not be offered the Torridge salmon and Stowe venison that the aristocratic Brothers of the Rose enjoyed 400 years ago, for such fare is still reserved for the wealthy, but they can share the ordinary fare of Salvation Yeo and his shipmates:

> For O! it's the herrings and the good brown beef,
> And the cider and the cream so white,
> O! they are the making of the jolly Devon lads,
> For to play, and eke to fight.†

The country people of Devonshire extend a warm welcome to the visitor, anyway at the beginning of the season. In May there is a sense of expectation. Farmers, village shopkeepers and garage proprietors look forward to renewing old friendships, and speculate on the takings. They have forgotten the vandals who wrote obscenities in the church visitors' book and the man who, when asked by the rector of Hartland not to smoke in church, replied, 'Why shouldn't I? It's a public place, isn't it?' But by August the fact that few visiting motorists bother to acknowledge a local driver who pulls into a gateway to allow them to pass; that the doctor's surgery is crowded out by people who have left 'Gran's tablets' behind, and that there is no space to park within a mile of the shopping centre begins to turn this welcome a little sour.

The best way to see the West Country is to travel out of season and on foot, as Kingsley so often did. The pleasure of walking in this area has been enormously enhanced by two bodies who would both have received Kingsley's support—the Countryside

---

* Letter from A. D. Hippesley Coxe to the author, March 1975.
† Traditional song quoted in *Westward Ho!*

Commission and the National Trust. The Countryside Commission has, as a result of much hard work and negotiation, established a footpath round the entire Cornish coast and is at present at work on the Somerset and North Devon Coast Path. These paths are, on the whole, well marked with little wooden signs bearing an acorn symbol.

The National Trust has also been very active in preserving this area. In March 1965 it launched Enterprise Neptune, recognising that the most pressing conservation problem facing Britain was to protect its remaining unspoilt coastline. A Trust survey showed that, of the 3,000 miles of coast around England, Wales and Northern Ireland, one-third was already ruined beyond redemption; another third was of no scenic importance, but the remaining thousand miles was of outstanding natural beauty and worthy of preservation for all time. A special campaign was launched to raise £2 million to protect this last thousand miles from haphazard building, badly sited industry and the spread of caravan sites. In the famous combes of the Far West, at least, these aims have been successful.

What pleasanter way to spend a fortnight than to set out from the western end of Kingsley's favourite stretch of coast, at Stowe, and walk to its eastern extremity at Appledore? We can start at Stowe Barton, the farm on the site of Sir Richard Grenville's famous house.* It is actually within a National Trust property of the same name, and its fine views up Coombe Valley to Kilkhampton are now safe for posterity. Of old Stowe all that can be seen is the moat which now encloses a beautiful seventeenth-century stone farmhouse, the home of Mr J. J. P. Hough. Coombe Valley remains the 'picturesque bottom' that John Murray described in his guide book of 1851. There is still a water mill and a miller's cottage in the valley; if the miller's cottage is the one in which Rose Salterne was imprisoned,

* The writer of the National Trust handbook is mistaken in supposing that Stowe Barton is on the site of Chapel of *Westward Ho!*

Kingsley was guilty of one of his not infrequent anachronisms, for both mill and cottage were built in 1842, probably with stones from Stowe. The mill, a three-storey building, was used until recently for grinding corn and its water wheel is one of the few still to be seen in the area. In Kingsley's time a wheel turned in almost every one of these western combes; by the beginning of this century most of them only dripped idly and now they are nearly all gone.

Kilkhampton church, mentioned in *Westward Ho!*, is much as it was, in spite of Sir Gilbert Scott's 'improvements' of 1860. It is justly famous for its Norman door of four richly decorated arches, although the Grenville tombs admired by Kingsley are, according to Pevsner, of 'indifferent quality'. The monument to Sir Bevil Grenville (who died in 1643, soon after his victory at Stamford Hill) bears an epitaph which refers to his father, the famous Sir Richard of *The Revenge*:

> Thus slain thy valiant ancestor did ly
> When his one Bark a Navy did defy

Kingsley would be pleased to know that the landlords of Coombe Valley,* far from excluding the common poeple, encourage them to enjoy it. A nature trail, opened in 1970 and administered by Cornwall's Naturalists' Trust, runs through the valley, commencing among the daffodils at the mill. Two gigantic white radar bowls desecrate the headland just north of Coombe and are visible for miles around. Because these alien objects in the landscape are part of the early warning system designed to protect his beloved island from her latter-day enemies—once again the Russians—Kingsley would surely forgive their intrusion. Admittedly, in themselves, they have a certain space-age beauty; they could even be taken for monstrous pieces of abstract sculpture. But they are totally at odds

---

* The National Trust, the Landmark Trust, Mr H. G. Hobbs and the Forestry Commission.

with the ancient farmsteads in the surrounding valleys, and the clutter of huts, car parks and concentration-camp wire that surrounds them is downright ugly. So is the crescent of houses nearby, built in directors' Georgian style to accommodate the men who service the installations.

From Coombe it is only 3 miles, travelling almost due north, to Tonacombe—the original of Chapel in *Westward Ho!* Tonacombe is a truly secret place that is best approached by a footpath. Owing to the understandable love of privacy of the family who have lived there for generations, very few people in recent years have seen inside it. Pevsner contents himself with remarking that it is 'modest and friendly', but a columnist in *The Times* in 1934 thought it 'worth crossing a continent to see'. This correspondent described the narrow courtyard as being of thirteenth-century origin and praised the medieval hall with its minstrel gallery and squint, 'whence the mistress of the house in her solar could discern the revelry of her lord'. Here, he also claimed, were preserved the rich curtains that once draped Sir Francis Drake's house, together with his day-bed. The present owner's great-grandfather, the Rev W. Waddon Martyn, claimed that the house was mentioned in an old deed of 1296, where it is described as 'the three vills of Tunnacombe'. It formerly belonged to the Jourdens and from them passed by marriage successively to the Leighs (alias Kempthornes), the Waddons, and then to the Martyns. Round the panelled drawing-room are the arms of the Leigh family.

Not the least of the mysteries at Tonacombe is the priest hole. At Chapel, the fictional version of the house, the Leighs not only hid priests in a secret chamber in one of the turrets but also heard mass in a chapel under the roof. The present owner, however, firmly denies that there was ever a priest hole, let alone a chapel at Tonacombe, and adds that the Leighs (or Kempthornes) who lived there in Elizabethan times were Protestant to the point of Puritanism.

Of a very different order of architecture is Morwenstow vicarage, close by the Norman church of St Morwenna in a daffodil-filled valley. It was built by Hawker, the poet-priest, and the chimneys are in imitation of the towers of the various churches with which he had been connected, the kitchen chimney being a reminder of his mother's tomb. There are memories too of 'Passon' Hawker in the churchyard. Strongly disapproving of wrecking (the chief source of income for his parishioners, and the inspiration of his *Cruel Coppinger* tales), Hawker befriended the shipwrecked sailor and, when he could not save him, at least afforded him decent burial in his churchyard. In 1842 he buried the captain and several of the crew of the *Caledonian*, a splendid brig of 200 tons from Arbroath. The ship's white figurehead stands above their grave, keeping her eye on the sheep which graze round it.

There is a footpath leading over the churchyard wall on to the windswept Vicarage Cliffs where Hawker built his hut. The hut is still there, just below the cliff top, looking out over a rocky cove of incomparable beauty, now the property of the National Trust. The walls of the hut, made from the timber of wrecked ships, are, alas, carved with many initials, but the visitor who sits on the bench at the back comes as close in spirit as he ever will to the two poet-parsons who sat there 125 years ago. Morwenstow is now a popular tourist attraction, with a car park and even an ice-cream kiosk above the church, but one suspects that few of the people who come there will walk across the 60 acres of glebe land to Hawker's hut.

From Vicarage Cliff, the footpath northward is clearly defined along the top of Cornakey Cliff. It is part of the Cornwall North Coast Path, walked by the occasional latter-day Muscular Christian. The two I met were American Mormon students, but no doubt in summer some of our own 'bulldog breed'* are to be met with. These cliff-top walks are not without their dangers,

* Charles Kingsley, *Two Years Ago*.

especially in a heavy mist or when strong offshore winds are blowing. The hardest part of the walk is the scramble down into the combes, and the scramble up the other side. Because there are so many changes in level, at least twenty-five per cent should be added to any distance shown on the map.

Marsland Mouth, where Rose Salterne waded out into the water at midnight, still marks the border between Cornwall and Devon. The rocks at low tide still run out to sea in parallel ridges and the strange cries of the sea birds still create an atmosphere in which one can half believe in magic. Fortunately, Marsland Mouth is likely to remain unspoiled as it is also the property of the National Trust.

Lovers of *Westward Ho!* should, at this stage in their journey, turn inland and follow the footpath that runs along the south side of Marsland Coombe, thus retracing the track of Eustace Leigh when he fled, wounded, from Clovelly over the moors. As they push their way through the undergrowth they may be lucky enough to stumble upon the lost foundations of the cottage of Lucy Passmore, Rose Salterne's white witch. According to Kingsley it 'remained as she had left it, and crumbled slowly down to four fern-covered walls'.* He probably based the character of Lucy on a witch called Temperance Floyd who had lived at Bideford in Elizabethan times. She was accused of making cows give blood instead of milk and was burnt at Exeter.

A little further up the combe is the old smithy which now dispenses food, drink and accommodation. In Kingsley's time it was still a forge, and Caleb Wakely, the last blacksmith, is remembered for pulling teeth as well as shoeing horses. Those who consider 8 miles of rough walking sufficient for one day might decide to spend the night here—it is at least 8 miles from

* There is some disagreement on this point. Ronald Duncan, the poet, who lives on the Cornish side of Marsland, at West Mill, and G. R. Marsh, who lives at Marsland Manor, on the Devon side of the border, each claims that the white witch lived in *his* house.

Stowe Barton by the coastal path, and the going is not made easier by gorse and brambles.

From Gooseham Mill, halfway up the combe, the bridlepath strikes northward to the grim tumulus-studded moors of Bursdon and Welford, over which Eustace fled by night and where the wind still rattles dismally through the dry ling, and the bogs are bottomless. Apart from house sparrows, the bird population of these moors has sadly declined since Kingsley's day, but a warm welcome can still be found at the West Country Inn at Bursdon. It was at this sixteenth-century coaching house that Kingsley stayed in 1849 when fishing the Torridge, which, like the Tamar, has its source nearby. The advertisements in the guides encourage us to eat, drink and be merry there, although the food is now limited to grills in the dining-room and chicken in the basket at the bar.

There are still fine trout to be caught in the Torridge, as Cyril Petherick, who owns a fishing tackle shop in Bideford, will tell you. Dace and gudgeon are also plentiful, but the famous salmon have been severely affected by a fatal skin complaint over the last five years. The disease appears to attack them when they leave the salt water of the sea (which is antiseptic) and come up river to spawn. The best salmon are caught upstream, between Beam Manor and the source of the river, but riparian rights are largely in the hands of private owners or local angling societies.

If we cannot catch a trout in the Torridge in Kingsley's memory, we can smoke a cigarette at this point. For it was not far from here that Salvation Yeo introduced Amyas Leigh to what was to become known as 'the Lotus leaf of Torridge'. They were travelling from Stowe to Burrough, and after ten miles of travelling, the one on horseback, the other at his stirrup, they were glad of refreshment. 'Yeo, in his solemn methodical way, pulled out of his bosom a brown leaf, and began rolling a piece of it up neatly to the size of his little finger; and then, putting the one end into his mouth and the other on the tinder, sucked at it till it was alight; and drinking down the smoke, began puffing it out again at his nostrils with a grunt of deepest satisfaction, and resumed his dog-trot by Amyas's side, as if he had been a walking chimney.'

At this stage it would be a pity to pursue Amyas and Yeo westwards for we would miss the magnificent north coast of the Hartland Peninsula. Better therefore to strike off northwards to Hartland church, where Kingsley preached on several occasions. Although St Nectan's is the parish church of Hartland, it lies two miles from the town, at Stoke. It is a cathedral-like church, befitting one of the largest parishes in England. Built in the fourteenth century on earlier foundations, it is famous for its rood screen, carved with flowers and shields, and miraculously overlooked by the commissioners of Queen Elizabeth. But most remarkable of all is its situation, looking across a mile of fields to the Atlantic. Its 130ft tower is the highest in Devon, and visible for miles around. Churches on its site have been beacons for seamen since the days of the Saxon Githa, mother of King Harold. From St Nectan's one can take the footpath that runs out to the cliffs to rejoin the coastal path.

Hartland Point is a terrifying experience in any weather. It was from this Promontory of Hercules that Kingsley, as a boy, sighted the ship in distress that finally sank on the Black Church Rock,* near Clovelly. It must have been catching the full force of the Atlantic gales on that day, but in fact on Harty Point, as the locals call it, the wind never seems to drop, and one has the uneasy feeling that even a large car parked near the edge might not be there when one returns. The whole cliff top is utterly bare and wind scorched, and it takes courage to creep to the edge (preferably on one's stomach) and look over. The resulting view is certainly rewarding. Ahead of you is nothing but a vast pile of water going on, presumably, until America;

* On modern maps the spelling is Blackchurch Rock.

beneath is the terrible black precipice of the cliffs, nearly 400ft deep.

While I was there I was lucky enough to see a school of porpoises pass by, far out to sea. Kingsley would have taken such a sight for granted. In his day he thought little enough even of a 40ft whale 'turning over in the water like a great black wheel'.* In 1927, when Henry Williamson published his famous book about the area, seals were common round Hartland Point and they can still be seen. Below the cliff is the cave where Tarka the Otter, and his mate Greymuzzle, dug for sand-eels and where dwelt Jarrk the seal and the white seal calf. Sea birds abound, and up on the bare summit of the headland are buzzards, ravens and the occasional peregrine falcon.

In only one respect has Hartland Point really changed since Kingsley's day: there is now a lighthouse there. Because of the appalling winds it is not, as one might expect, on the top, but halfway down the side, huddling on a ledge for shelter. It was built in 1874, a year before Kingsley died, and for its protection the summit of the headland had to be sliced off, a massive task. It has a fog horn which makes an ear-splitting racket in murky weather. In clear weather its light is visible from Tintagel and for a distance of 20 miles out at sea.

The six-mile route eastwards along the coast from Hartland is a scramble not a walk, but it is worth struggling over the steep indented Brownsham cliffs (now owned by the National Trust) to descend through lush semi-tropical vegetation to Kingsley's Mouth Mill. Here Will Cary proposed to keep watch for the popish invader, and here Kingsley himself admired the antics of the boys and girls who collected sand with the aid of pannier-carrying Exmoor ponies. The lime kiln, no doubt active in Kingsley's day, still stands.

The whole character of the coast changes once you round Hartland Point. The winds, although strong, are less violent,

* Charles Kingsley, *Madam How and Lady Why*.

and the ridges of rock which, on the west coast, ran straight out
to sea, now run parallel to the coast. At Mouth Mill they give
the impression of having been furrowed by some giant plough.
When the tide is out the deep pools between them are still
happy hunting grounds for naturalists.

From Mouth Mill beach you can clearly see the notorious
twin-arched Black Church Rock on which Kingsley's ship in
distress was finally wrecked. He would no doubt derive satisfaction from a latter-day feat of seamanship connected with the
'window rock'. In this century Sir James Hamlyn Williams's
grandson, Neville, sailed through it for a bet. Above the rock,
400ft Gallantry Bower is as beautiful as it always was and so is
the walk to Clovelly through the Deer Park woods.

Clovelly Court itself is still surrounded by open grazing land,
although the animals that graze it are no longer the famous deer
of Kingsley's day or even the red cattle of Edwardian times, but
a herd of sheep and a handful of retired hunters. The house
itself, despite a disastrous fire in 1945, retains some of the
features that Kingsley knew: the original main entrance still
stands, and the handsome nineteenth-century wing with the
Tudor part tucked away behind it. A descendant of Sir James,
the Honble Mrs K. Rous, lives there now. She is a great-niece
of his granddaughter, Mrs Christine Hamlyn.*

It was probably due largely to Mrs Hamlyn that Clovelly
remains unspoilt. 'The Queen of Clovelly', as they called her,
was born the year before Sir James died, and lived till 1936. She
was a tiny, sharp-faced woman with sparkling blue eyes and a
crown of white hair. The preservation and restoration of the
village (where many of the cottages now bear her initials) was her
passion, and she ruled the place with a rod of iron, or, to be
exact, a shepherd's crook. As she climbed up the steep cobbled
street in her flowing skirts she would point her crook accusingly
at an exposed rubbish bin, an unweeded flower bed or an un-

* Her husband changed his name to Hamlyn.

painted railing, and woe betide the householder who did not heed her warning. The morals of her tenants were expected to be as perfect as their premises, and laziness and drunkenness were frowned on. Their reward was an annual Christmas party in the servants hall at Clovelly Court, when Mrs Hamlyn would make a personal appearance in her diamonds, and distribute coals to the men, jumpers to the women and toys to the children.

Today Mrs Rous is the director of the discretionary trust established by her mother, Mrs Asquith, which continues to preserve Kingsley's 'steep stair of houses' from the vulgarity of our century. The population of Clovelly is only about a hundred, and although the first motor car attempted to climb the main street in 1920,* that was also the last. Clovelly is closed to wheeled traffic, but Land-Rovers use a track known as 'the back road' which runs down to the harbour just behind the Red Lion. Indeed the excellent beer that Roger Cann, a true West Country-man, dispenses there comes by this route. It was up this road that 400 donkey-loads of herring a day were carried when the fishing industry was at its height. Only a token service of donkeys with pack saddles now remains in Clovelly. But these donkeys will survive as long as the New Inn and the village shops halfway up the street continue to do business. Heavy goods going 'down-a-long' are put on sledges. The butcher and baker do their deliveries by toboggan. An interesting fact about the donkeys is that they do not carry tourists. A pre-war ruling of the Board of Trade insisted that each beast's burden should be weighed, and this proved too cumbersome a process when the burden was a human one.

Clovelly looks much as it did in Kingsley's day, and can still be reached by boat, although now this will be a small steamer owned by the White Funnel Line of Ilfracombe, and not a Clovelly trawler. The little harbour remains protected from north-east gales by the curved wall that encircles it like an arm,

* There is a photograph of the occasion in the bar of the Red Lion.

and the locals still sit and stare at you from benches outside the inn down by the harbour. The Red Lion is on the site of the three small cider houses that served fishermen in Kingsley's day. The cellars that stored coal (unloaded at the quay) have been converted into the bars of the hotel. From here the cobbled street tempts you upwards under the archway known as Temple Bar. This is in fact a house with a hole through it, and it was presumably in this house that Salvation Yeo, of *Westward Ho!*, son of an Anabaptist barber of Clovally—as the locals called it in those days—was born.

Kingsley would be sad to know that very few of its cottages are now inhabited by fishermen, for the herring shoals have migrated and there is no longer a living to be made from them—although the occasional Clovelly herring is still prized. One of the few remaining fishermen is Tommy Braund, a member of the famous Buck's Mills family—said to be descended from a shipwrecked Spanish sailor of the Armada. He is a Devon man after Kingsley's heart, sturdily independent and shunning publicity. He has a workshop in a loft where he makes seventy lobster pots every winter from Taunton black willow. When the spring gales are over, he lays them on the sea bottom and sells his catch at Plymouth, as his ancestors did before him.

Clovelly now subsists largely on tourism. In July and August not a single cobble of the famous down-a-long can be seen, for it is packed solid with people who appear to be standing in an endless theatre queue. A recent increase in the parking fees in the vast car parks above the village is unlikely to discourage the 9,000 visitors who come daily.

The person largely responsible for this tourist avalanche is none other than Charles Kingsley. It is he who must answer for the fact that almost every guide book to Devon has a colour photo of Clovelly on its cover and that china donkeys bearing the legend 'A present from Clovelly' are taken home by visitors from all over the world. Before he started to write about the place it was an unknown fishing village. Murray, in his *Handbook to Devon and Cornwall*, published in 1851, envisaged only the solitary traveller, who 'should rest a day at the little inn, which will entertain him with great hospitality'. A few years later C. S. Ward, author of *The Thorough Guide to North Devon and North Cornwall*, indicated that the rot had set in when he described it as 'a very paradise for the sketcher'. Another writer more crudely complained that there were 'artists and dustbins at every corner'. With the 1880s came what Murray, in a later edition, described as 'the flood of excursionists . . . disgorged from the excursion steamer down at the old pier . . . The picturesqueness of the place,' he declared, 'is not improved by cards announcing "hot water for tea" . . . which greet you at every step in the main causeway.' Murray was not pleased either by what he described as the garish Bideford pottery displayed in the shop windows, although now each piece would no doubt be a collector's item, for the two potteries where they were made have long since closed down.

This fate was not the one Kingsley had predicted for Clovelly in 1849, when he wrote his article on North Devon for *Fraser's Magazine*. 'It will not take another nineteen hundred years, to be sure, to make even this lovely nook as superior to what it is now as it is now to the little knot of fishing huts where naked Britons peeped out, trembling at the iron tramp of each insolent legionary from the camp above. It will not take another nineteen hundred years to develop the capabilities of this place,—to make it the finest fishery in England next to Torbay—the only safe harbour of refuge for West Indiamen, along sixty miles of ruthless coast—and a commercial centre for a vast tract of half-tilled land within, which only requires means of conveyance to be as fertile and valuable as nine-tenths of England.'

In Clovelly's defence, it must be pointed out that, even if it is not now a major port and commercial centre, it is not merely a resort. Out of season, it does not become a ghost town of closed shops and cafés. Brian Vesey Fitzgerald once described it as 'a sad little place that sits with its fingers crossed, hoping for one more coach than the day before', but Jeremy Thorpe, who represents it in parliament, firmly contradicts this description. Many of the people who live there, he points out, commute to Bideford and Barnstaple, and there is an active village life throughout the winter, centred on the well-appointed parish hall where church groups, the Women's Institute and, of course, the Liberals meet.

There is one change in Clovelly of which Kingsley, with his obsession about shipwrecks, would approve. In 1870 a shore-based lifeboat was subscribed for, and, during the hundred years of its existence, saved 350 people from the sea. In 1969 the RNLI introduced a new 'cruising lifeboat', the 70ft *70001*. She lies out in the bay and is always ready to move off in either direction along the coast to the aid of ships in distress. She runs for the shelter of Lundy Roads when the weather is bad.

The old rectory still stands above Clovelly, and it even contains a hunting parson. The Rev R. O. H. Eppingstone is a man after Kingsley's heart. Until recently, as priest-in-charge of Lundy, he made regular trips by boat to the island, and (weddings and funerals permitting), he is a familiar figure at meets of the local hunt mounted on his old horse, Jorrocks. The Stevenstone hounds (known as the North Devon in Kingsley's day) still hunt foxes—but not deer—over Bursdon and Welsford moors. Another keen member of the hunt is Mrs Waterman of Pierce's Farm Riding School at Broad Parkham. She supplies excellent hirelings for a gallop across the moors and through the forestry areas, and has introduced many children to the joys of riding on the Exmoor ponies so dear to Kingsley as a boy.

Kingsley would find more changes at Clovelly church than at the rectory, and would no doubt be flattered to find a brass memorial plate to himself on the wall. It was put there by his daughter, Mary, and her husband, the Rev William Harrison of Clovelly, who was Kingsley's last curate, and a great admirer. Indeed one suspects that it was Harrison rather than his wife who was responsible for the plaque, for Mary regarded her father as old-fashioned to the point of naïveté. Shortly after the tablet was erected she parted from Harrison and set herself up as an advanced lady novelist.

Another obvious change in the church is the stained glass. In 1885 the omnipresent Kempe filled the east window with three tiers of small figures, and in 1898 similarly embellished the west window. In the churchyard Kingsley would be pleased to see that his brother Henry's nursemaid is not forgotten. A tombstone to Susannah Blackmore of Parracombe declares that she died in 1889, still in the service of a rector of Clovelly.

Above the village, Clovelly Dykes are almost exactly as they were when Father Campian and Father Parsons were surprised there by the Brothers of the Rose. The three concentric earthworks, surrounded by an outer embankment, give a fine view from the highest point. There is no sign of those marks of twentieth-century approval—a car park and a Ministry of Works ticket kiosk. The only visitors to the wide green terraces are a flock of sheep.

If we are following faithfully in Kingsley's footsteps, we should make our visit to Lundy from Clovelly, as he did. This can be done by those who own a boat, but others must go from Ilfracombe by White Funnel steamer or, in the Kingsley tradition, the 20-ton trawler *Gannet* or the *Polar Bear*. There is no air service to Lundy, which is still a proper island, not tamely linked to the mainland by a helicopter shuttle-service. Nor is it an island you can land on in all weathers. If the wind is in the east the ship will circle the 500ft-high coast and bring you back frustrated to the mainland. Lundy has, however, compromised with the twentieth century to the extent of installing a radio-telephone, while the agent, Ian Grainger, has a Land-Rover (which has not been universally welcomed).

Lundy has passed through several hands since Kingsley sat above Shutter Rock and imagined Don Guzman drinking wine beneath the sea. Until the end of the last century it remained in the hands of the Heaven family who had owned it since 1834, and Edwardian boatmen would alarm their passengers by announcing, 'Ladies and gentlemen, we are now nearing the Kingdom of Heaven!' as they approached the harbour. The death in 1969, of the last private owner, Albion Harman, left lovers of Lundy in a state approaching panic. There were rumours that it was to be taken over for a top security prison; that it would be turned into a holiday camp; that the Scientologists would have it, or the tax dodgers or the casino owners. It was at this stage that a coalition of three local members of Parliament, Jeremy Thorpe, Peter Mills and David Owen, set about saving the island for the nation. As a result of their efforts, Mrs Harman accepted an offer of £150,000 donated by a Bahama businessman, Jack Hayward, although she had had higher bids from elsewhere. The island is now owned by the National Trust and administered by the Landmark Trust, through a resident agent.

The only building of any size to go up since Kingsley's day is St Helen's church, built by the Rev Hudson Grosett Heaven in 1896, to hold a congregation of 400. It was designed by J. Norton, the architect of many town churches, which explains its somewhat urban appearance. Lundy has no rector of its own, but is cared for by the vicar of Appledore. The Rev Noel Peyton Jones, a retired naval officer who dresses like a Greek Orthodox bishop, is a man admirably suited to the task. His visits to the island usually last several days, during which time he camps out in the vestry. As he also does his cooking there, the congregation at evensong can usually deduce what he had for lunch. When the vicar is absent, Ian Grainger, the agent, conducts the service. The present Bishop of Exeter had encouraged him to continue with his 'Presbyterian form of religion', which suggests that the present occupant of the episcopal chair is more broadminded than the man who filled his position 120 years ago.

Kingsley was right in his prediction about the lighthouse in the centre of the island. It proved useless because it was so frequently obscured by fog, and it has now become a centre of pilgrimage for our faithless but antique-loving generation, as he said it would. Its place has been taken by the North and South lights.

The number of day visitors to the island has increased to 30,000 a year, and for people who want to spend the night there is more accommodation than ever before. The Harmans' rhododendron-shrouded house, Millcombe, on the way up from the harbour, is now a hotel with fifteen beds. Several cottages have been converted for holidaymakers, and there are plans to restore a ruined barn and roundhouse as a hostel. None of this has spoiled the essential character of the desolate island which is divided into sections by the ancient quarter, halfway and three-quarter walls (built in part by the convict slaves of a former owner, the notorious Benson). The southern quarter, where the boats land beneath Marisco Castle, remains the only inhabited part. Off the south-western tip of this section stands the notorious Shutter Rock, although no ship has been wrecked on it since the 14,000-ton HMS *Montagu* went aground in 1906. (She lies there submerged to this day.) Those with stomachs for it can look down into the booming Devil's Limekiln nearby. It is 370ft deep and 250ft wide at the top, linked to the sea by caves. Its sides are vertical granite and loose stones shift beneath your hands and knees as you crawl towards the edge.

Moving northwards up the island, the animals, like the land-scape, become wilder. In the second quarter there are sheep, cattle and deer, in the third wild ponies (introduced since Kingsley's day) and more deer, and in the fourth nothing but wild goats and Soay sheep—and seagulls. Lundy is still a bird-watchers' paradise. The great auk no longer nests there, as it did in Kingsley's early boyhood, but the cliffs are alive, not to say discordant, with sea-birds. Perhaps the best place to watch them is the western cliffs which, although slightly lower than the eastern ones, are more precipitous. Here you can look down on guillemots, razorbills, kittiwakes and gannets, literally in their thousands. From above these birds take on a different aspect from the familiar one. The gannets, for instance, look like torpedoes pointed at both ends, with long black-tipped wings. The gulls are noticeably neckless by comparison with them.

But for those who wish to see puffins a bitter disappointment is in store. The birds which gave the island its name—'Lundy' means puffin—and which appear on Harman's Lundy stamps, have gone, or almost gone. Twenty-five years ago they could be seen in their hundreds, sitting outside their burrows like aldermen in striped pyjamas, stupefied with corporation port. Now you are most unlikely to see one.

One reason for their decline is certainly oil pollution. Kingsley would have been appalled at the numbers of seabirds dying of exposure because their feathers, clogged with crude oil, are useless. The problem is even worse on the mainland. Even when kind-hearted local people like Mrs Katherine Tottenham of Instow, clean them, they often perish because their feathers are no longer waterproof, or because of the quantity of oil they have swallowed. The birds most subject to contamination are the divers, such as guillemots, shearwaters and puffins, which cannot see the oil to avoid it, when they come up to the surface.

Much of the slick that reaches the coasts of Devon and Cornwall comes from the Azores. The oil is voided by ships cleaning their fuel tanks or by tankers cleaning out their holds, and is wafted towards Britain's shores at a rate of twelve miles a day. Were Kingsley still with us he would no doubt throw his reforming energy into demanding international action. Although laws exist against this vile practice, at present there is no means of enforcing them.

Fewer than forty people live permanently on Lundy and none of them have roots there. They will have to face huge financial problems in the near future if they are to maintain the island in its present form; £100,000 could be spent right away merely on repairs to the existing buildings, and a small village would need to be built to house the workmen for such a task. At a meeting of the Torridge District Council's Development Committee in February 1975 it was agreed that a programme lasting at least ten years would be necessary if Lundy were to remain habitable.

Returning from Lundy a really competent sailor could no doubt land at Freshwater, where Eustace Leigh came ashore by moonlight. The waterfall still splashes on to the pebbly beach at this point, half a mile east of Clovelly, and it is still possible to scramble to the top. Although there is no path, a pleasant surprise awaits the climber, for the Hobby Drive* now skirts these wooded cliffs. It is so called because it was the hobby of Sir James Hamlyn Williams in later life. Kingsley probably never saw the Hobby because it was built after he left Devonshire, but he would certainly have appreciated it, for he could never sufficiently praise previous improvers who made the road through the Deer Park woods, on the other side of Clovelly. 'Those who first thought of cutting it,' he once declared, 'must have had souls in them above the common herd.'† From one of the moss-grown bridges of the Hobby it is possible to look straight down the glen that terminates in Freshwater cascade, where Amyas and Frank Leigh lay in wait for Eustace. The vegetation here is as luxuriant as it ever was, and the variety of ferns is amazing. There are also breathtaking aerial views of Clovelly Harbour.

On leaving the Hobby the admirer of Kingsley should take the cliff-top path to Buck's Mills and Peppercombe and then strike inland to meet the Torridge once more at Weare Giffard. The

* The road is private; cars are charged 30p and must approach from the Bideford end.
† Charles Kingsley, *Prose Idylls*.

reason for this manoeuvre is that the Torridge is navigable up to this point so it is possible to approach Kingsley's beloved Bideford by boat. The first place one would expect to see, as one floated downstream, would be Annery, gazing at its own reflection from its promontory on the left bank. But the old house, in whose grounds Will Cary and Don Guzman fought their famous duel for Rose Salterne, was demolished around 1960, after standing empty and derelict for many years. A bungalow now stands on the site; another structure that Kingsley would not recognise is the railway bridge at the confluence with the Yeo.

Seen from a boat, Bideford Bridge does not appear to have changed at all in the last 120 years. From the river you cannot see that it is wider than it was in Kingsley's day, just as then it was wider than it had been in Amyas Leigh's. The Elizabethan bridge allowed only the passage of pack ponies. Over each pillar, angles were provided into which pedestrians might take refuge when animals were crossing. Since the widening of the bridge in 1925 the continuous traffic of the A39 to Barnstaple can pass with ease in both directions. The bridge also bears another and more precious burden, the famous 'hot line' to America; when part of the bridge was swept away in 1968, the line was temporarily severed.

Bideford Quay, like Bideford Bridge, has been continuously widened since the days of Amyas Leigh. According to W. Crosbie Coles,* author of *Kingsley's Country*, a guide published in 1893, the quay that Amyas Leigh knew was not a quarter of the width of the present one. On the other hand, none of the houses along the quay existed then, apart from the Rose of Torridge Café—formerly the Ship Tavern.† In their place was a stretch of waste land covered in part by low thatched sheds and warehouses. According to Crosbie Coles, it was the houses of

---

* A former owner of the *Bideford Gazette*.
† It has always been assumed that the Brotherhood of the Rose was formed at the Ship Tavern.

Allhalland Street that overlooked the river in those days. Of these the finest was always said to be Sir Richard Grenville's town house, with gardens running down to the quay. By the time the rector of Eversley came to the town, the Steam Packet, the King's Arms and the Three Tuns were keeping the Ship Tavern company,* thus narrowing the quay which nevertheless remained adequate for the quiet little place that Bideford was in 1854.

It was only after the immense success of *Westward Ho!* that 'the pleasuring public', as the author of *Kingsley's Country* described them, began to beat a path to Bideford, on their way to Clovelly. By 1892 'the frequent congestion of traffic on the river front amounted to a positive danger', and the quay was built out into the river and planted with an avenue of trees. As if acknowledging his responsibility for these improvements, Kingsley himself stands at the end of the new quay, perpetuated in marble and robed in his professorial gown.† He was no doubt gratified when, in January 1975, in honour of the centenary of his death, the mayor of Bideford and a local paint manufacturer scrubbed off the homage that generations of seagulls had paid him.

Yet, in spite of its expansion, the town has not changed beyond recognition. Kingsley would be pleased to see Dr Ackland's house in Bridgeland Street still standing. He would be less pleased to see the twin-spired Independent Chapel nearby, built four years after he left. There is still a shop at 28 Mill Street, where Edward Capern, the poet-postman, lived; it now sells cassettes, not vegetables. And Northdown Hall remains, although not in its former splendid isolation, for part of its garden forms a sports ground, while its coach house and stable block are used for a motor repair business. Kingsley would no

* The Steam Packet is now the office of a building society and the Three Tuns, which was formerly the home of Sir Bevil Grenville, houses a gas board showroom.

† The statue was unveiled in 1906 and lost the nib of its pen to local hooligans shortly afterwards.

doubt be somewhat surprised to find that the house itself is now a Catholic convent, where the nuns of the order of Stella Maris run a school for 500 girls. The original building is somewhat obscured by recent additions, and the little corner bedroom where Kingsley wrote the paragraphs against popery in *Westward Ho!* is said to have been used as a chapel for a time.

Another building in Bideford that has changed, perhaps not entirely for the better, is St Mary's church, down by the bridge. It was rebuilt in 1864, except for the tower. The famous monument to Sir Thomas Graynfyldd of 1513 was preserved, however, and in 1891 a new memorial was put up which would have pleased Kingsley. A brass tablet to Sir Richard Grenville was placed there by his descendant, the Rev Roger Grenville, to commemorate the 300th anniversary of his death. A child bored by the sermon can take a lesson in English history from it that Kingsley would be happy for him to learn:

About the 4th of September AD 1591 died of his wounds on board the Spanish Galleon the Sante Paule, off the island of Flores, in the Azores having in HMS The Revenge endured in a fifteen houres fight the assault of fifteen severall Armadoes, all by tournes aboorde him, and by estimation eight hundred shot of great artillerie beside manie assaults and entries

Sir Richard Grenvile Knight Vice Admiral of England aged 48

His last words spoken in Spanish were these

Here die I, Richard Grenvile with a joyful and quiet mind for that I have ended my life as a true soldier ought to do, fighting for his country, Queen, religion, and honour, my soul willingly departing from this body leaving behind a lasting fame of having behaved as every valiant soldier is in duty bound to do. A Fight Memorable even beyond credit, and to the height of some heroicall fable.

Kingsley himself is not forgotten at St Mary's. On the Sunday nearest to the centenary of his death—26 January 1975—a memorial service for him was held there at the suggestion of the Rev Gilbert Molesworth, who also arranged for services to be held at Northam, Alwington, Heanton and at Westminster

Abbey itself. Molesworth, a grandson of the Captain George Molesworth who rented Northdown Hall to Kingsley, lives in a charming old cottage on the banks of the Torridge estuary where the high spring tides lap the stems of the daffodils.

Bideford is proud of all aspects of its history, and in 1973 it celebrated with due pomp the quarter centenary of its attainment of borough status. Two local residents composed a song about how Bideford Bridge had withstood the assaults of Philip of Spain, Napoleon and Hitler,* and this was sung by Geoffrey Savage, who farms Rectory Farm, at Morwenstow, just outside Parson Hawker's gate. There will be no further such celebrations. As a result of local government reorganisation Bideford has become a ward of the Torridge District, its council is now a parish council and its mayor no more than a 'town mayor'.

'The little white town on the hill' is not merely a tourist centre or a place to retire to. Although few boats are tied up at the quay now, and these are coastal craft, there is an active shipbuilding industry. The Bideford Shipyard at Bank End has a history of industrial relations of which Kingsley would approve. When it went into liquidation in 1973 as the result of the bankruptcy of its parent company, the men offered to work for nothing until a buyer came forward. Kingsley might find two of Bideford's other industries less to his liking. Although the plastic baby pants made by Dri-Troo and the gloves stitched at Sudbury Gloves Ltd are neither cheap nor nasty,† and the people who make them work under good conditions, Kingsley was never happy about light industry. He once wrote, 'I conceive it a very great evil that large bodies of men should be employed in exclusively performing, day after day, the same minute mechanical operation, till their whole intellect is concentrated on it, and their fingers kept delicate for the purpose.'

---

* Bideford played a special part in the 1939–45 war. The Normandy landings of 1944 were planned by high ranking officers based at East-the-Water.

† Kingsley wrote a pamphlet entitled *Cheap and Nasty* about the appalling working conditions of tailors in 1850.

The working people of Bideford would not agree with him. They would like to see more rather than less industry in their town, for unemployment is higher than elsewhere. As Jeremy Thorpe pointed out in an interview with the author, when England catches cold Devonshire contracts pneumonia. Yet Bidefordians do not wish to see the character of their little town changed. A few years ago, they bitterly—and successfully— opposed a scheme to settle London's overspill between East-the-Water and Barnstaple. In fact a 45,000 increase of population by natural growth is expected in the county before the end of the century.* Because of housing development, East-the-Water is less attractive than Bideford proper. Indeed the only buildings worth crossing the bridge to see are Chudleigh Fort (Cromwellian) and the Royal Hotel, which still preserves its famous upper room.

Kingsley would be glad to know that the arts, as well as industry, flourish in Bideford. An art school, such as he attempted but failed to establish, stands at the end of the quay, opposite his statue. Its premises are also used by Bideford Community College, which is one of the most advanced centres of adult education in the country. Under the direction of a warden, an adult tutor and two youth tutors, its work goes far beyond that of an ordinary evening institute, and it acts as a vitalising and integrating force for the whole area. According to Nigel Melville, the adult tutor, 'the process is bringing the college into touch with people whom we would not ordinarily meet',† in other words, working people. Kingsley, who took a keen interest in the founding of the London Working Men's College in 1854, could not but be pleased.

The education of the young is not neglected either, and Kingsley, who campaigned for the advancement of women, would be glad to know that girls are, if anything, better served

* Report of South West Economic Planning Council, 1974.
† Letter from Nigel Melville to the author, 10 March 1975.

at Bideford with two public schools (Edgehill College and Stella Maris Convent), whereas there is only one for boys (Grenville College). Kingsley might, however, have some reservations about Edgehill College being a Methodist foundation.

In the public sector there are six primary schools, and two secondary, of which one is the old Bideford Grammar School, about to go comprehensive. At the time that Kingsley lived in the town the school was all but defunct* and the number of pupils did not go above a hundred till after World War I. The school moved to its present premises, in Abbotsham Road, in 1935. In recent years it has expanded considerably.

The people of Bideford are keen sportsmen, and Kingsley's statue has a ringside view of the annual rowing regatta, held on 13 September, which brings Bidefordians home from all over the world. It is the last, and best, of the West of England competitions and attracts top crews. When the local football team ran out of money in 1966 there was a massive community effort to put it on its feet again. Almost every car passing over Bideford Bridge seemed to display a 'Save our football' sticker.

As a postscript to this survey of modern Bideford, it should be added that—to quote the guide of 1893—'a thorough system of sewage was carried out in 1871 at a cost of £4,000, and that the "zymotic death rate" [that is to say, death from infectious diseases] was down to ·984 in the thousand'. Modern guide books do not tell us whether this system has been extended, but, judging by the clean streets and the healthy appearance of the inhabitants, we may assume that it has, and certainly there has been no cholera in Bideford this century.

One of the most beautiful walks out of Bideford is that which Amyas and Frank Leigh took to Appledore, in pursuit of the perfidious Eustace. It starts at the Kingsley statue, passes Vic-

---

* In 1868 a Parliamentary inquiry announced that the Grammar School consisted of nineteen pupils being instructed over a cellar 'in which a cooper practises his trade'.

toria Park (where several small cannon of the Armada period stand in a circle) and follows the river for most of its three and a half miles. The Mariner's Rest Inn, where the Leighs watched the Jesuits attempting to mount their horses, is now a private house, but in the old part of Appledore little else has changed. The narrow 'drangs' run steeply up the sides of the hill, and the Georgian houses with their studio windows still stand along the quay. These are now colour washed, so that Kingsley could no longer describe the place as a 'little white fishing village'.

Appledore today boasts not one but two shipyards. Appledore Shipbuilders Ltd, founded the year *Westward Ho!* was published, produce an average of ten new ships a year, including ocean-going tugs and auxiliary naval vessels. In their new covered yard, opened in 1970, two 5,000-ton ships can be built side by side. Perhaps more to Kingsley's liking would be the smaller yard owned by J. Hinks and Son, which specialises in the construction of wooden sailing vessels. It was here that the full-size replica of Sir Francis Drake's *Golden Hinde* was built, destined for San Francisco to commemorate Drake's landing there 400 years ago. And in Appledore they do not just play at war. In the early 1940s there was a naval establishment here of 1,000 men, and troop carriers sailed from the little quay for the North African landings.

It is an uphill walk from Appledore to Northam, and the reward is small for a lover of Kingsley country. Burrough, the home of Amyas Leigh, was swept away by philistines of the last century, soon after Kingsley wrote about it, and by 1868 had been replaced by the present substantial but graceless Victorian house. Northam church suffered desecration at about the same time. Around 1865 the 'restorers' covered over all the Leigh memorials. True, one can still stand outside the porch and imagine the burial of Salvation Yeo. They laid him in view of the sea in case 'the old man might like to . . . see the ships come in and out across the harbour'. But to enjoy his vigil Yeo must

ignore all that has in the meantime grown up between the sea and
Northam—what was once a beautiful view is filled with ill-
placed bungalows. Kingsley is not entirely ignored at Northam;
the inn sign of the Kingsley Inn, Fore Street, portrays Amyas
Leigh, with sword in air, being struck blind by a flash of
lightning.

Northam Burrows is not as extensive as it was when Kingsley
knew it. The pebble ridge has gradually been forced back by the
sea, and much of what he knew as grazing land is under sand.
Part of this submerged area was excavated at the end of the last
century, and a pair of antlers and some of the fossilised remains
of a buried forest are preserved at the Barnstaple Athenaeum.
One of the oldest and most famous golf clubs in England, the
Royal North Devon, has the Burrows for its links, but Kingsley
would probably prefer the parts that are still remote. These are
best described by Henry Williamson in the winter scenes from
Tarka, when the sedges and reeds of the duck ponds were white,
and the thousand tracks of small animals and birds criss-crossed
the pans and plains like the veins of a leaf. The pebble ridge was
breached and the greater part of the Burrows, including the golf
course, submerged during the severe gales of early 1975. A
£75,000 scheme is now afoot to build twelve groynes of pebbles,
held together with wire mesh. Perhaps if the pot wallopers had
continued to do their annual duty of throwing up stones on to
the ridge this money could have been saved.

And so, sadly, we come to Westward Ho!, the place that
Kingsley could never bring himself to visit, and for which he is
indirectly responsible. It stands partly on the cliff at the western
end of the Burrows, and partly on the Burrows themselves, and
nobody, apart from the writers of highly coloured holiday
brochures, has a good word to say for it. 'A tatty kind of Mar-
gate,' said Ray Gosling in the 1950s; 'A sad spectacle of what un-
controlled speculative building can do,' said W. G. Hoskins in
the 1960s. The addition of a dozen or so self-catering 'chalet

estates' and 'caravan gardens' has done little to improve its appearance in the 1970s.

At first sight there appears to be no memorial to Kingsley at Westward Ho! The writer who receives all the attention is Kipling, to whom the famous 'wuzzy' of Stalky and Co—24 acres of gorse-covered cliff top—is dedicated. Visitors who search diligently, however, will discover a row of tall yellow brick houses that was once Kingsley College. It stands almost next door to the terrace of houses that was Kipling's United Services College, now under threat of demolition. Both buildings have been converted into holiday flatlets.

The history of Kingsley College is a brief one. In 1884 a printed announcement declared that a new college, in memory of the Late Rev Charles Kingsley, had opened, and was to be dedicated to Mrs Charles Kingsley (at that time still living). It went on: 'KINGSLEY—household word, especially in North Devon. As a lecturer and teacher there was a fascination in manner, a force in imparting knowledge, which few acquire. He possessed great powers over university students and schoolboys; he laboured also among the humbler classes. No more fitting place than Westward Ho! for a memorial to this great good man; no more suitable object than a college for one so devoted to education.'

Kingsley College consisted of two terraces of houses, connected by means of a churchlike building, topped by a spire, which housed the dining hall, gymnasium and chapel. The school aimed to provide the sons of clergymen, lawyers and doctors with the advantages enjoyed by the pupils of the United Services College. Coats-of-arms of the college, representing the professions for which it prepared its sons, are discernible under many layers of paint on the iron railings in Kingsley Road. The college used to be known as the Irish College because it was founded at a time of trouble in Ireland, and its pupils came mainly from Portarlington. It closed, for reasons that are obscure, after only four years. Perhaps the Irish parents were unable, or unwilling, to pay the fees. The gymnasium now houses the town's community centre.*

When Kingsley lived at Bideford, Westward Ho! did not exist. The pebble ridge was still the lonely windswept place where Amyas Leigh 'sniffing the keen salt air like a young sea dog, stripped and plunged into the breakers'. The only dwellings to be seen were a few farmhouses and 'Underborough', a gentleman's residence. Two of the farms, Venton and Commons, are still standing, and the farmhouse of a third, Youngaton, built in 1750 is now the Grenville Arms.

It was in 1863 that the Northam Burrows Hotel and Villa Co Ltd was formed to develop the district as a resort. The prospectus of the company, published in the *Bideford Gazette*, opened with the following words: 'The recent publication of Mr Kingsley's charming work, *Westward Ho!* has awakened public interest in the romantic and beautiful coast of North Devon.' The most active of the directors of the new company was Captain Molesworth, Kingsley's landlord at Northdown Hall. The fourth son of a Lancashire vicar, he was a big landowner and a JP whose Tory principles had often clashed with those of his former Christian Socialist tenant. Molesworth was above all things a businessman of immense energy and enthusiasm, and was the moving spirit behind every venture at Westward Ho!—whether it was the ladies' swimming bath, the pier, the railway, the golf club, the gasworks or the colleges.

It was Molesworth's ambition to make of Westward Ho! a fashionable watering place that would surpass Ilfracombe and even rival Torquay. The names of rich and titled people about to visit the town began to appear in the local paper, but they never seemed to materialise, and one suspects that Captain Molesworth merely hoped they were coming. His ambition to

---

* I am indebted for much of this information to Ronald Mayo, author of *The Story of Westward Ho!*

provide Westward Ho! with a pier was also frustrated. The 600ft structure was almost complete when disaster struck; an October gale snapped the cast-iron pillars 'just like tobacco pipes'.

It was not Molesworth, however, who had the idea of calling the new resort Westward Ho! The inspiration was that of Kingsley's old friend, Dr Ackland, also a director of the company. Kingsley never disguised his abhorrence of the project. In a letter to Ackland in 1864 he summed up his attitude to villa development in North Devon. 'How goes on the Northam Burrows scheme for spoiling that beautiful place with hotels and villas? I suppose it must be, but you will frighten away all the sea-pies and defile the Pebble Ridge with chicken bones and sandwich scraps. The universe is growing cockney, and men like me must look out for a new planet to live in, without fear of railways and villa projections.'

Perhaps he has found, in that Other World that he so longed to inhabit with Fanny, an idealised version of North Devon as it was before the developers came.

Selected List of Works of Charles Kingsley

1848	*The Saint's Tragedy*
1849	*Alton Locke*
1849	*Yeast*
1849	*Twenty-five Village Sermons*
1852	*Phaeton*
1853	*Hypatia*
1855	*Glaucus*
1855	*Westward Ho!*
1856	*The Heroes*
1857	*Two Years Ago*
1858	*Andromeda and other Poems*
1859	*Miscellanies*
1860	*The Limits of Exact Science applied to History* (Inaugural Lecture)
1863	*The Water-Babies*
1866	*Hereward the Wake*
1869	*The Hermits*
1869	*Madam How and Lady Why*
1871	*At Last*
1873	*Prose Idylls*

Index

143